Systematic synthetic phonics: case studies from Sounds-Write practitioners

Edited by Ana Beaven, Anna Comas-Quinn, and Naomi Hinton

Published by Research-publishing.net, a not-for-profit association
Contact: info@research-publishing.net

© 2022 by Editors (collective work)
© 2022 by Authors (individual work)

Systematic synthetic phonics: case studies from Sounds-Write practitioners
Edited by Ana Beaven, Anna Comas-Quinn, and Naomi Hinton

Publication date: 2022/05/09

Rights: the whole volume is published under the Attribution-NonCommercial-NoDerivatives International (CC BY-NC-ND) licence; **individual articles may have a different licence**. Under the CC BY-NC-ND licence, the volume is freely available online (https://doi.org/10.14705/rpnet.2022.55.9782383720010) for anybody to read, download, copy, and redistribute provided that the author(s), editorial team, and publisher are properly cited. Commercial use and derivative works are, however, not permitted.

Disclaimer: Research-publishing.net does not take any responsibility for the content of the pages written by the authors of this book. The authors have recognised that the work described was not published before, or that it was not under consideration for publication elsewhere. While the information in this book is believed to be true and accurate on the date of its going to press, neither the editorial team nor the publisher can accept any legal responsibility for any errors or omissions. The publisher makes no warranty, expressed or implied, with respect to the material contained herein. While Research-publishing.net is committed to publishing works of integrity, the words are the authors' alone.

Trademark notice: product or corporate names may be trademarks or registered trademarks, and are used only for identification and explanation without intent to infringe.

Copyrighted material: every effort has been made by the editorial team to trace copyright holders and to obtain their permission for the use of copyrighted material in this book. In the event of errors or omissions, please notify the publisher of any corrections that will need to be incorporated in future editions of this book.

Typeset by Research-publishing.net
Cover layout by © 2022 Laura Walker

ISBN13: 978-2-38372-001-0 (Ebook, PDF, colour)
ISBN13: 978-2-38372-002-7 (Ebook, EPUB, colour)
ISBN13: 978-2-38372-000-3 (Paperback - Print on demand, black and white)
Print on demand technology is a high-quality, innovative and ecological printing method; with which the book is never 'out of stock' or 'out of print'.

British Library Cataloguing-in-Publication Data.
A cataloguing record for this book is available from the British Library.

Legal deposit, France: Bibliothèque Nationale de France - Dépôt légal: mai 2022.

Table of contents

v Notes on contributors

xv Foreword
   Pamela Snow

1 Introduction
   John Walker and Tita Beaven

11 Allambie Heights Public School, Sydney, Australia
    Angela Helsloot

23 Angel Oak Academy, London, England
    Charlotte MacKechnie

31 Bloomfield Learning Centre, London, England
    Sarah Horner and Jane Orr

43 Docklands Primary School, Melbourne, Australia
    Emina McLean

55 Johnson STEAM Academy Magnet School, Cedar Rapids, Iowa, USA
    Katie Eichhorn, Kathy Gilbert, Myra Hall, Gretchen Lawyer, and Jill Nunez

63 Merllyn Community Primary School, Bagillt, North Wales, United Kingdom
    Tracy Jones

71 Nollamara Primary and Intensive English School, Perth, Australia
    Kendall Hammond

79 Princecroft Primary School, Warminster, England
    Anita Harley

87 Selby Community Primary School, North Yorkshire, England
    Emma Darwin

Table of contents

97   Speech-language therapist, Munich, Germany: one-to-one intervention
Shelley Hornberger

105   St George's Church of England Primary School, London, England
Alexandra Hammond

113   The Pavilion School, Melbourne, Australia
Naomi Stockley, Rianna Tatana, Roshni Kaur, Alice Reynolds

125   Glossary

131   Author index

Notes on contributors

Editors

Ana Beaven works as a language teacher at the University of Bologna, Italy. She has a doctorate in applied linguistics and publishes in the fields of intercultural language learning and teaching. She has co-edited several collections of case studies related to language education and virtual exchange.

Anna Comas-Quinn is Research and Development Lead at Sounds-Write. She has a doctorate in education and spent nearly three decades working in academia, most recently as a senior lecturer at The Open University, UK. She researches and publishes on education and language learning and has co-edited two collections of case studies by education practitioners.

Naomi Hinton is Head of Training at Sounds-Write. Before joining the Sounds-Write team, Naomi taught and led across the primary age range in two National Support Schools – she was an assistant headteacher in London before moving to Yorkshire where she taught phonics both in the classroom and as an intervention.

Invited author

Pamela Snow is Professor of Psychology in the School of Education at La Trobe University, Australia. She is a registered psychologist, having qualified originally as a speech-language pathologist. Her research is concerned with oral language competence in childhood and adolescence and optimal reading instruction and support across the school years.

Authors

Tita Beaven is Director of Innovation and e-learning at Sounds-Write, instructional designer of the Sounds-Write online courses and author of many

Notes on contributors

teaching resources, including some of the Sounds-Write decodable readers and activity books. She has a doctorate in educational technology and 25 years of experience as an academic at The Open University, UK, where she designed online and distance courses at undergraduate and postgraduate level.

Emma Darwin lives in the beautiful city of York, North Yorkshire, and is a teacher with extensive experience in early years and most recently in Primary KS1. Emma is now leading phonics across a two-form entry school, supporting the delivery of the Sounds-Write programme throughout EYFS/KS1 alongside interventions in KS2.

Katie Eichhorn has been a special education teacher for the last thirteen years in Cedar Rapids, Iowa, where she teaches students from third to fifth grade at Johnson STEAM Academy. She was Sounds-Write trained in the spring of 2020 and, since using Sounds-Write, has had many success stories with at-risk students and those who need additional support with reading.

Kathy Gilbert has been an educator with the Cedar Rapids Community Schools District for over twenty years and a reading specialist at Johnson STEAM Academy for eight years. Her passion is teaching young, at-risk children the joys of reading and helping them become lifelong learners.

Myra Hall works as a literacy consultant at Grant Wood Area Education Agency in Cedar Rapids, Iowa. During her 35 years as an educator, Myra has worked as a classroom teacher, special education teacher, administrator, professional development provider, coach, and consultant. Myra is particularly interested in action research and innovations to support effective teaching and student learning.

Alexandra Hammond is the Reception Teacher and Early Years and Key Stage One Leader at St George's Church of England Primary School. Alexandra has a Bachelor of Arts in early childhood development and worked in primary schools in Sheffield and Manchester before moving to London. She is an avid reader and enjoys sharing this passion with the children she teaches.

Notes on contributors

Kendall Hammond is Associate Principal at Nollamara Primary School in Perth, Western Australia. She is passionate about explicit instruction with literacy and is leading the change at the school in curriculum and pedagogy.

Anita Harley is the Year 1 teacher at Princecroft Primary School, one of the Sounds-Write training schools in the UK. She is a senior leader, leading on phonics and writing across the school. She was one of the first Princecroft teachers to be trained in Sounds-Write and has been teaching it across KS1 for five years.

Angela Helsloot has been the Principal of Allambie Heights Public School, Sydney, Australia, for ten years. She has taught in primary schools for 25 years, many of these in the first three years of formal schooling. She is a strong advocate for teaching phonics both in the classroom and as an intervention.

Shelley Hornberger is a speech-language therapist and currently runs an independent speech-language therapy practice for English-speaking children and young people in Munich, Germany. Her areas of clinical interest include developmental language disorder and associated written language difficulties in school-age children, as well as bilingualism.

Sarah Horner has worked as a specialist teacher for many years, teaching students who find developing literacy skills challenging. She currently teaches in a state primary school, where she is also Phonics and Spelling Lead, and at the Bloomfield Learning Centre, both in London, England. She has been a Sounds-Write trainer since 2005.

Tracy Jones is a headteacher at Merllyn Primary School in North Wales. She has a teaching career spanning nearly 30 years in both England and Wales. She is also involved at a national level in developing assessment and progression processes within the new curriculum for Wales.

Roshni Kaur holds a Bachelor of Speech Pathology, completed in 2016. Roshni has experience in education settings and currently works at The Pavilion School

Notes on contributors

twice a week. She also has experience working in private settings and in a mental health setting for children and adolescents.

Gretchen Lawyer is Equity Coach with the Cedar Rapids Community School District in Cedar Rapids Iowa and was the Propel Literacy Implementation Coach at Johnson STEAM Academy in Cedar Rapids from 2017-2021. She has been an educator for 15 years serving in classroom teaching, reading interventionist, and coaching roles.

Charlotte MacKechnie works for the STEP Ahead Teaching School Alliance as Senior Lead for Teacher Development and is a specialist leader of education for phonics, English, and leadership of continuing professional development. She became a Sounds-Write trainer after using Sounds-Write in the classroom and leading the implementation of a whole-school approach to teaching reading and spelling using Sounds-Write at Angel Oak Academy in London.

Emina McLean's background is in speech pathology, education, child and adolescent psychiatry, and public health. She is an English, literacy, and pedagogy researcher and lecturer, and Head of English and Literacy at Docklands Primary School. Emina also works as a professional learning provider, consultant, and instructional coach in schools across Australia.

Jill Nunez is Instructional Coach at Johnson STEAM Academy in Cedar Rapids, Iowa. She has been in education for seventeen years and her primary areas of interest are literacy and equity.

Jane Orr, MA (Oxon), PGCE, RSA Dip (Spld), is headteacher of the Bloomfield Learning Centre, a charity providing specialist assessments and tuition for children struggling with reading and spelling. As a primary teacher in South London, she witnessed the seemingly insurmountable difficulties some pupils suffered whilst learning to read, prompting her to train as a specialist dyslexia teacher and to eventually adopt Sounds-Write.

Notes on contributors

Alice Reynolds is Learning Specialist and Classroom Teacher at The Pavilion School in Melbourne, Australia. In this dual role, she takes a keen interest in the development and implementation of effective teaching and learning programmes to improve academic outcomes for marginalised students. Alice considers quality education to be a key protective factor for young people, particularly those who have experienced trauma.

Naomi Stockley completed the Teach for Australia Leadership and Development Programme in 2017, and began her career in education as a Spanish teacher. Her passion for language, evidence-based practices, and working with disengaged students led her to apply for a job at The Pavilion School. She received training in Sounds-Write and played an integral role in establishing and coordinating the whole-school phonics intervention programme. She still works at The Pavilion School as a classroom teacher and acting Campus Coordinator.

Rianna Tatana is a proud Widjibul Wia-bul Bundalung and Māori woman. She is an educator who has worked across both mainstream and alternative high-school settings for six years. She co-developed and co-coordinated the Phonics Programme at The Pavilion School. Her aspiration is to support first nations and at-risk young people seeking access to equitable education.

John Walker is the director of Sounds-Write and one of the co-authors of the programme. He has been a qualified teacher, university lecturer and teacher trainer for over 30 years. He has presented regularly at ResearchED conferences and was appointed as a 'reading expert' on the English Hubs Council at the Department for Education in the UK. John blogs on all aspects of literacy teaching at theliteracyblog.com.

Reviewers

Faith Borkowsky is the founder of High Five Literacy and Academic Coaching with over 30 years of experience as a classroom teacher, reading and learning

Notes on contributors

specialist, regional literacy coach, administrator, and tutor. She is a certified dyslexia practitioner and the author of the award-winning book, *Failing Students or Failing Schools? A Parent's Guide to Reading Instruction and Intervention* and the '*If Only I Would Have Known...*' series.

Derrie Clark is Chartered Child and Educational Psychologist specialising in literacy and behaviour. His professional doctorate looked at literacy development and assessment. He has been a trainer in Sounds-Write since 2005.

Miriam Fein is a US-based speech-language pathologist and licensed reading specialist. She lives near Boston, Massachusetts, and provides individual and small group intervention to students from early elementary grades through high school in the areas of reading, spelling, writing, and language skills.

Tarjinder Gill is an experienced primary school teacher who has worked in socio-economically deprived areas in London, Great Yarmouth, and the Midlands. She specialises in history and English. She contributes to the national conversation by participating in ResearchEDs, the Festival of Education, and the Battle of Ideas.

Pam Heath has considerable teaching experience in both primary and secondary, and has worked closely with pupils encountering literacy difficulties. Most recently Pam was a school improvement adviser and Special Education Needs and Disabilities (SEND) and Vulnerable Pupils and Phonics Lead, providing guidance and support on improving SEND and phonics outcomes in schools. Pam has delivered the National SENCO Award and has been a Sounds-Write trainer for over twelve years.

Shelley Hornberger is a speech-language therapist and currently runs an independent speech-language therapy practice for English-speaking children and young people in Munich, Germany. Her areas of clinical interest include developmental language disorder and associated written language difficulties in school-age children, as well as bilingualism.

Notes on contributors

Sarah Horner is an experienced teacher and Sounds-Write trainer, with qualifications in assessing and teaching students with specific learning difficulties. She currently teaches in both mainstream and specialist settings. Since becoming a Sounds-Write trainer in 2004, she has combined teaching children with reading difficulties with training teachers and support staff in the Sounds-Write programme.

Amy Hulson-Jones is Honorary Senior Associate, Lecturer, and Research Officer at the School of Educational Sciences, at Bangor University, Wales, UK. Amy is also a qualified primary school teacher and divides her time between researching effective instructional methods and putting them into practice within the classroom.

James Lyra is a Sounds-Write trainer and a registered early childhood teacher and paediatric occupational therapist who has worked as a classroom teacher, occupational therapist, and literacy specialist and curriculum coordinator at one of the largest high schools in Western Australia. James is director of Rise Literacy, where he provides specialist literacy intervention services in the Canberra region to students aged four to thirteen years.

Tricia Moss is Trust Curriculum Lead at the Diocese of Ely Multi-Academy Trust. She supports schools in all aspects of curriculum pedagogy. She holds an MEd (Cambridge) specialising in the teaching of reading and is a Sounds-Write practitioner. Before joining the teaching profession, Tricia was an editor and publisher.

Emma Nahna is a New Zealand-based Speech-Language Therapist who provides professional learning and development to schools and early childhood settings, supporting them to embed evidence-informed, effective literacy and oral language teaching for all learners.

Andrew Percival is a deputy headteacher at Stanley Road Primary School in Oldham, UK. He has been teaching in schools for over twenty years and currently

Notes on contributors

leads on curriculum development and English. Andrew has delivered training on developing a knowledge-rich curriculum to over 200 schools across the UK.

Alison Perry is a speech-language pathologist and Sounds-Write trainer based in Brisbane, Australia. She is the founder of Soundality and has a passion for educating others to better understand how to effectively teach reading and spelling, particularly to children with learning disorders and difficulties.

Theresa Plummer worked in Scotland and The Netherlands before settling in London, where she worked for 27 years at St George's Church of England Primary School. As a senior specialist teacher, she was responsible for implementing Sounds-Write and ensuring all students achieved age-appropriate literacy by the age of seven. She is now a full-time Sounds-Write trainer.

Allison Potter (MA in education and MA in literacy learning and difficulties) is an English adviser in the NE, supporting schools with early reading, phonics, comprehension, and reading for pleasure. She also works for the National Literacy Trust as Hub Manager, supporting disadvantaged communities to discover the power of books.

Maria Richards is a former primary school teacher, subject leader, and leading literacy teacher. Maria was part of the Somerset School Improvement Service, working with schools to raise attainment. She is now a freelance English consultant and an accredited member of the Talk for Writing team, working with Pie Corbett.

Sue Russell is based in the South of England and has been a Sounds-Write trainer for over ten years and has trained over 3,000 staff in that time. Other roles have included primary class teacher; parenting support and training; delivery of the extended services agenda; and supporting and advising parents of children with special education needs and disabilities to obtain their children's legal entitlement to education.

Reid Smith is a primary teacher and the Head of Curriculum at a school in regional Australia and has taught for two decades. Reid is a PhD candidate at the La Trobe Science of Language and Reading Lab, studying the relationship between knowledge availability and reading comprehension in primary-aged children.

Marion Storey has taught across the primary stage, mainly with the youngest children in EYFS and Year 1. As well as being a full-time class teacher she was SENDCO and English Coordinator with responsibility for developing reading and writing across the school and improving outcomes for all children. She has shared evidence of success with other schools across her local authority.

The Reading Ape writes about reading.

Gurjit Virk has been a headteacher for seven years and is currently the head of a large three-form entry primary school in Bedford. Gurjit has introduced Sounds-Write in both schools she has led and has seen the positive impact that the programme has had on the children within her schools.

Foreword

Pamela Snow[1]

In the third decade of the 21st century, it is difficult to think of an aspect of children's education in industrialised, first-world nations that is more important, yet sadly, more contested, than reading instruction. Ironically, reading and how to teach it, is also one of the most widely researched aspects of child development. A number of branches of psychology, such as cognitive, experimental, educational, and developmental neuropsychology have devoted hundreds of thousands of hours to outputs in academic journals and research theses, conference presentations, blogs, social media posts, and private and public debates. The publication of three national inquiries (the US in 2000, Australia in 2005, and England in 2006) heralded something of a false dawn in putting the major debates to rest, unanimously highlighting the importance of an early focus on explicitly and systematically teaching children (as readers and writers) how the English writing system works, alongside supporting their development in phonemic awareness, vocabulary, fluency, and comprehension.

As readers of this volume will know, the recommendations of these inquiries have had somewhat troubled lives. In the US and Australia, selective quote-mining gave renewed life to so-called 'balanced literacy', the love-child of whole language and a 1980s zeitgeist of child-led, discovery-based learning. For a range of reasons, however, England's recommendations, most notably the mandating of systematic synthetic phonics instruction, made it out of the pages of a government report and into classrooms, notwithstanding some resistance that persists to this day.

Robust recommendations are one thing, but robust implementation of those recommendations is something else altogether. This is why schools need access

---

1. School of Education, La Trobe University, Bendigo, Australia; p.snow@latrobe.edu.au

How to cite: Snow, P. (2022). Foreword. In A. Beaven, A. Comas-Quinn & N. Hinton (Eds), *Systematic synthetic phonics: case studies from Sounds-Write practitioners* (pp. xv-xvi). Research-publishing.net. https://doi.org/10.14705/rpnet.2022.55.1353

to high-quality programmes that have the heavy-lifting already done in terms of their theoretical foundations, scope and sequence, teaching materials and scripts, assessment and monitoring tools, high-quality training and coaching, and demonstration videos. Sounds-Write is such a programme, and it is no surprise that its developers have gone the extra nine yards to compile this collection of case studies about how Sounds-Write looks in action.

What is notable about these case studies is their diversity. You will read about schools and specialist literacy settings from a range of nations: England, Wales, Australia, Germany, and the US. Some are in extremely disadvantaged urban communities; some are schools with high proportions of children from homes where English is an additional language. Then there are schools with large numbers of students receiving disability-related funding, and a school providing a 'last-chance' at education for adolescents who live in out-of-home care, are involved in the youth justice system, and have complex emotional and behavioural sequelae associated with years of academic failure, shame, and embarrassment. Many settings tick several of these boxes in fact. No, this is not a report of a Randomised Controlled Trial (RCT), because funding for those is scarce, and by definition, RCTs would exclude the types of messy, real-world contexts you will read about here (and probably work in yourself).

The commonality between these settings is a belief on the part of teachers that *their students can learn to read*, and that it is their instruction, not the characteristics of the students, that determines whether this happens. The authors of the case studies acknowledge the challenges they encountered (not the least of which, in recent times, was the COVID-19 pandemic) and discuss how these continue to be managed. These Sounds-Write case studies are accounts of objective examination of student data, commitment to staff training, fidelity of implementation, focused use of communities of practice and targeted professional learning, and celebration of what in all cases was a data-based uplift in the learning trajectories of their students. Changing outcomes for students embodies the Holy Grail of research knowledge translation and I hope policy makers, school leaders, university academics, and classroom teachers will reflect on the power of these accounts and what they could mean if taken to scale.

Introduction

John Walker[1] and Tita Beaven[2]

If you're reading this book, it's probably because you want to know what evidence base there is for using Sounds-Write with your students. You might already be familiar with our approach to teaching phonics and want to hear from other practitioners how they've implemented it in their schools, or you might indeed be new to Sounds-Write and want to find out more about it. Whatever your background, in this book you'll find a collection of case studies in which practitioners share their experiences of implementing the programme and their recommendations on how to do it successfully.

1. Why this book?

We are often asked for evidence of the effectiveness of Sounds-Write.

When we first developed the approach and the programme in 2003, we were keen to evaluate its effectiveness, so from 2003-2009 we conducted a longitudinal study of the literacy development of over 1,600 students in Key Stage 1 (the first three years of school). That study tracked students from Reception to Year 2 using Young's *Parallel Spelling Tests*[*3] to ascertain the spelling ages of the students year on year. Data showed that, including the students who scored below but within 6 months of their actual age level (252 students), a grand total of 1,463 out of the 1,607 students in the study were in a position to be moving up to Year 3 with basic literacy skills at an age-appropriate level, or above. This amounts to 91% of the students in the study.

---

1. Sounds-Write, Buckingham, United Kingdom; john@sounds-write.co.uk

2. Sounds-Write, Buckingham, United Kingdom; tita@sounds-write.co.uk; https://orcid.org/0000-0002-9074-8789

3. An explanation for terms followed by an asterisk can be found in the glossary: https://doi.org/10.14705/rpnet.2022.55.1367

How to cite: Walker, J., & Beaven, T. (2022). Introduction. In A. Beaven, A. Comas-Quinn & N. Hinton (Eds), *Systematic synthetic phonics: case studies from Sounds-Write practitioners* (pp. 1-9). Research-publishing.net. https://doi.org/10.14705/rpnet.2022.55.1354

Introduction

Since we conducted that initial study, Sounds-Write has expanded and is being used in many different contexts, both in schools and in clinical settings by speech and language therapists and specialist reading tutors, as well as in different countries (UK and the rest of Europe, Australia, New Zealand, USA, and Canada, to name the main ones).

As requests for evidence kept coming, in 2020, we decided that it would be useful to share the stories of practitioners who had implemented Sounds-Write through a collection of case studies. We decided to focus on case studies as they would provide a lot of in-depth, granular data about how Sounds-Write is used in specific settings. From a methodological point of view, the case studies use a range of instruments to evaluate the effectiveness of Sounds-Write, and this is a reflection of the huge variety of settings in which Sounds-Write is being used. Because of this variety, the case studies elucidate different aspects of the effectiveness of Sounds-Write which, when pulled together, tell the story of how Sounds-Write can be best implemented and the impact it can have.

Working with practitioners who are not researchers also means that we had to work with the data that schools had gathered for their own needs, rather than commissioning them to gather data following our own specifications. Being practitioners rather than researchers also meant that the authors of the case study often went beyond their comfort zone when writing up the data. We would like to thank the authors and also our wonderful editors, Ana Beaven, Anna Comas-Quinn, and Naomi Hinton, who supported and guided them through the process and helped them find their voice, and our peer reviewers, who provided detailed feedback on the drafts. We would also like to thank Professor Pamela Snow, not only for writing the foreword to this volume and for her support over the years, but also for her valuable and continuous work advocating for the Science of Reading.

2. Gathering data in the middle of a pandemic

As soon as we started planning this volume, the world – and the education sector – was turned upside down because of the global pandemic. We wondered whether to stop work on the volume and put it off until things 'got back to normal', but decided to continue with the project. We are glad we did, in the sense that the case studies reported here illustrate the difficulties schools and practitioners faced when education was disrupted by lockdowns, and the creative ways in which they tried to overcome them. They also reflect the reality of the massive disruption caused by the pandemic to the education of many students, especially in the early years when the teaching of reading and spelling is so crucial.

The data of some of the case studies show the effect of the pandemic on the students' progress. We could have discarded that data and only presented data gathered before the pandemic struck, but we felt that would be methodologically dishonest, and that it was much more ethical to present the data for the COVID years too, 'warts and all'.

We would like to thank all the schools and educational organisations that were involved in these case studies and, in particular, the authors of the case studies for their willingness to share their experiences. More importantly, we want to pay tribute to all the educators who have worked tirelessly to continue supporting their students' literacy development through these difficult times.

3. What is Sounds-Write?

If you are not familiar with Sounds-Write, here's a very brief outline.

Sounds-Write is an approach to the teaching of reading and spelling based to a large extent on the work of Professor Diane McGuinness[4], Emeritus Professor of Psychology at the University of South Florida.

---

4. Diane McGuinness is the author of many research papers, but see in particular:
McGuinness, D. (2006). *Early reading instruction: what science really tells us about how to teach reading.* MIT Press.
McGuinness, D. (1997). *Why our children can't read, and what we can do about it: a scientific revolution in reading.* Simon and Schuster.

Introduction

It is a direct instruction approach based on the Science of Reading and incorporating insights from Cognitive Load Theory[5], and provides scripted lessons for educators to deliver with consistency and rigour.

The most crucial aspect of Sounds-Write, however, is that it is a sound to print approach: it starts from what all children learn naturally, the sounds of their language, and teaches them how to represent those sounds in writing. Although some people may think this is just a small quirk of our approach, it is key to everything we do because it provides us with a conceptual framework elucidating the relationship between the sounds of the English language and the writing system.

3.1. Code knowledge, skills, and conceptual understanding

Through a carefully crafted sequence, Sounds-Write introduces learners to one-to-one correspondences first through what we refer to as the Initial Code*, and then moves on to teach the complexities of the English alphabet code through the Extended Code*. At the same time, we train students to be proficient in the skills needed to read and write effectively, namely segmenting, blending, and manipulating phonemes, and we also teach them explicitly the conceptual knowledge that is essential to make sense of the English alphabet code:

- letters are symbols that represent sounds and are written from left to right across the page;
- sounds can be represented by one, two, three, or four letters;
- we can spell sounds in more than one way; and
- many spellings represent more than one sound.

Finally, we also teach that the code is reversible: if you can read it, you can spell, and vice-versa, so Sounds-Write is an approach to the teaching of both reading and spelling.

---

5. Sweller, J. (1988). Cognitive load during problem solving: effect on learning. *Cognitive Science, 12*(2), 257-285.

3.2. Adjacent consonants and polysyllabic words

Many phonics programmes don't spend time teaching the skills of segmenting and blending adjacent consonants at all; if they do, they don't teach the skills robustly enough; or, they postpone teaching these skills until much too late, leaving many students floundering when confronted by words with adjacent consonants. When introducing the Initial Code, we do this through Consonant Vowel Consonant (CVC) words, but then spend considerable time training students to decode and write words of greater structural complexity: CCVC, CVCC, CCVCC, CCCVCC, etc.

Similarly, after students start on the Extended Code, we introduce strategies to read, write, and analyse polysyllabic words, and focus on morphology and etymology in the context of expanding the students' vocabulary.

3.3. Error correction

Teaching through errors is an important aspect of the Sounds-Write approach. Indeed, mistakes provide an excellent opportunity for teaching and learning: most teaching and learning takes place when the learner encounters a problem they have to solve and where the teacher steps in to provide guidance. Research also shows that feedback is most effective when it is delivered immediately, while the error is still fresh in the mind of the learner. When errors are made, immediate feedback also helps to prevent students from continuing to make the same error and thus make it become 'fossilised'.

When a student makes an error, some teachers supply the correct answer and solve the problem for them. This robs the students of the opportunity to analyse what the 'difficult bit' for them is in any particular word and to focus on just that thing. It also robs the teacher of the opportunity to find out what exactly it is the student has difficulty with. As far as is possible, we point the student in the right direction so that they can solve the problem for themselves, helping them to develop into independent learners.

3.4. Precise, simple, and honest language

Educators are often told to say things like 'this letter makes the sound…' or use terminology such as 'silent letters' or 'magic e'. We say that letters don't make sounds – we do – that all letters are silent (try putting your ear to a book and you'll 'hear' that they are very quiet indeed!); and that there's nothing magical about learning to read and write. It's a logical, albeit complex, process, and we use precise, simple, and honest language to explain how it all works, so that students are taught in a way that is consistent, straightforward, and honest.

3.5. Teacher knowledge is key

You'll see that a lot of the authors of the case studies mention the fact that training all staff has been a key factor in their successful implementation of Sounds-Write. Research shows that teacher knowledge is one of the most important factors in teaching and learning, and that is why Sounds-Write is fundamentally a training-based approach rather than a resource-based programme.

We strongly believe that if educators have a good understanding of how the writing system works and how to teach it, and they follow the approach with fidelity, they can achieve success and help their students to learn to read and write.

We hope you enjoy reading the case studies in this volume and that you find them informative and useful.

What you will find in this book

This collection of case studies comprises twelve very different accounts of how Sounds-Write is used successfully to teach reading and spelling in schools and other educational settings.

Angela Helsloot, Principal at **Allambie Heights Public School**, on the Northern Beaches of Sydney, uses data from standardised tests and benchmark reading assessments across the school to show the positive impact that Sounds-Write instruction has had in Kindergarten and Year 1.

Charlotte MacKechnie reports on improvements in reading and spelling for all children at **Angel Oak Academy** in South East London following the adoption of Sounds-Write. They use a three-teacher model to support small-group and one-to-one 'keep up' interventions to ensure children are not left behind in their phonics learning.

Sarah Horner and Jane Orr from the **Bloomfield Learning Centre**, a specialist literacy clinic run as a charity and serving the poorest parts of London, report on how Sounds-Write helped a student regain his self-confidence and motivation for learning, after difficulties in reading had led to behaviour problems and a dislike of school.

Docklands Primary School opened its doors in Melbourne in January 2021. Emina McLean, Head of English, describes how Sounds-Write was implemented in Foundation to Year 2 in the middle of the pandemic. Despite four lockdowns forcing periods of online teaching, various standardised tests show 80% of students on average meeting or exceeding expectations.

Katie Eichhorn, Kathy Gilbert, Myra Hall, Gretchen Lawyer, and Jill Nunez from **Johnson STEAM Academy** in Cedar Rapids, Iowa, share data showing improved reading results after their first year of implementation of Sounds-Write, including a successful partnership with a local middle school to use Sounds-Write with Grade 7 students who were up to four years below grade level.

Introduction

At **Ysgol Merllyn**, a primary school serving the village of Bagillt in North Wales (UK), Tracy Jones, Headteacher, presents data from diagnostic assessment used to determine how well children had retained knowledge of the Extended Code during the disruptions posed by lockdowns and periods of remote learning.

Kendall Hammond, Associate Principal at **Nollamara Primary and Intensive English School** in Perth, explains how their commitment to explicit direct instruction made Sounds-Write a natural choice for the teaching of reading and spelling in a school where three-quarters of students have English as an additional language.

Anita Harley, Phonics Lead at **Princecroft Primary School** in the rural town of Warminster in the UK, describes how a focus on teacher development and using Sounds-Write with fidelity has resulted in increased attainment in phonics and spelling for children, the vast majority of whom now meet or exceed expected standards.

Prior to implementing Sounds-Write in 2016, phonics attainment in Year 1 at **Selby Primary School** in North Yorkshire (UK) was at or above the national average, but little progress was made by the weaker readers by the end of Key Stage 2. Emma Darwin, Phonics Lead at the school, presents data for a Year 4 cohort who have been taught using Sounds-Write from Reception.

As a **speech-language therapist** supporting English-speaking students from international schools in Munich, Germany, Shelley Hornberger shares the story of a student referred after many years of failed school and private phonics instruction. She reports significant progress made by this student, in spite of having to deliver the programme online for extended periods during the pandemic.

St George's Primary, in Battersea, south London, began using Sounds-Write in 2011. Alexandra Hammond, current Key Stage 1 and Phonics Lead, presents spelling test data to illustrate progress and achievement for a group of twenty students from Year 1 to Year 6.

Naomi Stockley, Rianna Tatana, Roshni Kaur, and Alice Reynolds offer some early insights into the implementation of Sounds-Write at **The Pavilion School**, a specialist provision in the northern suburbs of Melbourne for vulnerable students who have been excluded from mainstream education and face significant personal challenges.

To help you make sense of what may be unfamiliar terms or concepts, given the global nature of the examples included, we have added a glossary at the end of the book. Terms that appear in several case studies have been included in the glossary and are indicated in the text with an asterisk, whereas footnotes have been used to provide additional information related to individual case studies.

Each case study is divided into four sections. The **'Context'** provides general information about the setting and should make it easier for readers to locate relevant examples. In the **'Implementation'** section, the process of introducing and supporting the adoption of Sounds-Write is described. Next is the **'Evaluation'** section, where data on the impact that Sounds-Write has had on attainment in reading and spelling is presented and discussed. Though tests and measures vary from one country and context to another, we hope each case study tells a clear story of success and improvement in literacy for the students who have experienced Sounds-Write.

At the end of all case studies, authors draw on their own experiences to share some **'Recommendations'** for practitioners who are considering using Sounds-Write. Authors concur on the importance of implementing the programme consistently and with fidelity, and of supporting practitioners' professional development. At the heart of this is high-quality training for all staff involved in the delivery of phonics, but also the need to continue developing practice through reflection, coaching, and peer support, and by taking advantage of the additional training opportunities, resources, and support available for those who join the Sounds-Write community.

1 Allambie Heights Public School, Sydney, Australia

Angela Helsloot[1]

1. Context

Allambie Heights Public School is located on the Northern Beaches of Sydney, New South Wales, Australia. It is a Kindergarten*[2] to Year 6 school for students aged five to twelve years. The school is

> "committed to the pursuit of high academic achievement in a safe, secure, and caring learning environment. The programs offered are diverse, and challenge and inspire our students. Students, parents and staff work in partnership to create a vibrant learning community. Literacy, numeracy and technology are emphasized within learning programs"[3].

The school motto, 'Ever Aim High', "underpins the school's strong belief that each child needs to be recognized for their own achievements, celebrating success [both at] a school and personal level"[4]. As a Positive Behavior for Learning school, the school values of respect, responsibility, and resilience are key to the success of our school community. We currently have 514 students and 51 staff in our school. Four students identify as Aboriginal and Torres Strait Islander and 14% of students come from a language background other than English. The school is in a high socio-economic area with a Family Occupation and Education

---

1. Allambie Heights Public School, Allambie Heights, Australia; angela.helsloot@det.nsw.edu.au

2. An explanation for terms followed by an asterisk can be found in the glossary: https://doi.org/10.14705/rpnet.2022.55.1367

3. https://myschool.edu.au/

4. https://myschool.edu.au/

How to cite: Helsloot, A. (2022). Allambie Heights Public School, Sydney, Australia. In A. Beaven, A. Comas-Quinn & N. Hinton (Eds), *Systematic synthetic phonics: case studies from Sounds-Write practitioners* (pp. 11-22). Research-publishing.net. https://doi.org/10.14705/rpnet.2022.55.1355

© 2022 Angela Helsloot (CC BY)

Chapter 1

Index[5] (FOEI) of 17. The school Index of Community and Socio-Educational Advantage* is 1,112.

2. Implementation

In 2017, as a school leadership team, we evaluated different synthetic phonics programs as part of writing our 2018-2020 school plan. From analyzing NAPLAN (National Assessment Program – Literacy and Numeracy*) and school data we recognized that we needed to increase the number of students in Year 3, Year 5, and Year 7 achieving in the top two bands and demonstrating expected growth in NAPLAN reading and writing. Our research led us to understand that there is strong "evidence that systematic synthetic phonics, taught in the first years of a child's education, gives children [the] building blocks they need to read and understand words, [and supports] children's attainment of a [high] standard of reading"[6]. Furthermore, we could see from examining Scarborough's Reading Rope[7], the need to improve our teaching of the word-recognition strand. This led us to evaluate different synthetic phonics programs and to choose Sounds-Write. Sounds-Write was the program selected by our leadership team because of its use of explicit direct instruction, which is best suited to our morning literacy focus that encompasses guided, modeled, and independent learning. The progression and pace of the Sounds-Write teaching sequence was also more favorable than the other programs reviewed as it could be incorporated into classroom teaching and learning and support programs.

Sounds-Write became a key program in our 2018-2020 school plan with the commitment to train teachers and implement the program from Kindergarten to Year 3.

---

5. The FOEI is a school-level index of educational disadvantage related to socio-economic background. FOEI values range from 0 to approximately 300, with higher FOEI scores indicating higher levels of need (that is, lower socio-economic status).

6. http://docplayer.net/25181924-A-practical-guide-to-synthetic-phonics.html?

7. https://dyslexiaida.org/scarboroughs-reading-rope-a-groundbreaking-infographic/

We started our Sounds-Write journey in 2018. During that year, twenty staff members across the school including the Principal, Deputy Principal, and two Assistant Principals attended the 4-day face-to-face training. Implementation of the program began in learning and support programs from the beginning of 2018 and from Kindergarten to Year 3 classes in Term 3. Training continued in 2019 for all Kindergarten to Year 3 teachers.

A scope and sequence* was developed from Kindergarten to the end of Term 3 of Year 3 to teach the Initial* and Extended Code* and introduce polysyllabic words. Full implementation across all Kindergarten to Year 3 classrooms and Kindergarten to Year 6 learning and support programs started in the 2019 school year. All Kindergarten to Year 3 classes have four 20-25 minute Sound-Write sessions a week. Further support has been given to identified students through additional Tier* 2 and Tier 3 interventions using Sounds-Write. These small group and individual withdrawal lessons have a twenty-minute focus on Sounds-Write and a twenty-minute focus on reading comprehension and fluency.

By the end of the 2020 school year, 42 staff across the school had completed the Sounds-Write training course. To ensure consistency across the school, all new teaching staff train in Sounds-Write. With current Covid-19 restrictions, staff now train online. This consistency allows staff and students to utilize the potential of the program to benefit all learners. Additionally, in 2020, three teachers completed the refresher course to review and improve the delivery of Sounds-Write. Teachers felt this course helped to support their confidence and deepened their knowledge of teaching Sounds-Write. The refresher course also led to deeper discussions between Kindergarten to Year 2 staff about the transfer of sound knowledge from short-term memory to long-term memory for recall, particularly with spelling. These discussions led to a change in practice regarding the review and assessment of sounds in retrospect to determine this transfer of knowledge.

Our future goal is to extend our use of Sounds-Write to improve the way we teach spelling and vocabulary in Year 3 to Year 6. In 2020, the first group of six teachers completed the 'Teaching Vocabulary in Year 3 to Year 6' course, and in 2021 a further six teachers completed this training. We are now revising our Year 3 to Year 6 scope and sequence and developing a bank of lessons to accompany this scope and sequence to ensure a consistent approach for all students in all classes.

3. Specific case study

The 58 students in this case study are currently in Year 2, 2021. They are our first cohort who have followed the Sound-Write program since they started Kindergarten in 2019. This is their third year of following the program. During this time all students have received four 20-25 minute whole-class Sounds-Write sessions a week.

Further support has been given to identified students through the Sounds-Write learning and support program. In this program, four identified students attend a 40-minute small group session Monday to Thursday. This small group of students have a 20-minute focus on Sounds-Write and a 20-minute focus on reading comprehension and fluency.

3.1. 2019 – Kindergarten

Across the year, ten students (17%) attended additional Sounds-Write support lessons in Kindergarten. Four students benefited from one term of support, three students had two terms of support, one student had three terms of support and two students had four terms of support. The students attending the support program in Kindergarten consolidated Initial Code units, which had previously been taught during the classroom program.

Moving into Year 1, seven of these students required continued Sounds-Write learning support, two students did not require further learning support after Kindergarten, while one student was withdrawn from the support program by parents as they do not believe learning support is essential. This student continued their development of phonics through the class Sounds-Write sessions.

3.2. 2020 – Year 1

Across the new school year, seven original support program students attended additional Sounds-Write support sessions in Year 1. They were joined by a newly enrolled student who had not been exposed to a synthetic phonics approach at their previous school. This equates to 12% of the cohort attending learning support. Three students benefited from one term of support, three students had two terms of support, one student had three terms of support, and one student had four terms of support. The students attending the support program in Year 1 consolidated the bridging unit and Extended Code units, which had previously been taught during the classroom program.

During the first Covid-19 lockdown in March-May 2020, which forced schools to be closed for seven weeks, we continued to teach Sounds-Write sessions to the whole class and to intervention groups through Zoom sessions and recorded videos. Although not as intensive, results at the end of the year showed that students had continued to make expected progress in reading and spelling.

Moving into Year 2, three of these students required continued Sounds-Write learning support, four students have transitioned to a broader literacy support program, and one student did not require further learning support after Year 1.

3.3. 2021 – Year 2

Across the new school year, three original support program students attend additional Sounds-Write support lessons in Year 2. This equates to 5% of the cohort attending Sounds-Write learning support. Three students benefited from three terms of support, two terms of face-to-face support, and one term of online support through Zoom and recorded videos due to the whole of Term 3 being in a Covid-19 lockdown. The students attending the support program in Year 2 consolidate the Extended Code units which have previously been taught during the classroom program.

Our Sounds-Write learning support program is funded by two department-funded positions – Learning and Support Teacher and Literacy and Numeracy Intervention Teacher (previously specified as Reading Recovery). Combined, the teacher is employed four days per week and was one of our first teachers trained in Sounds-Write in 2018.

Our future plans include the implementation of a Year 4 to Year 6 program, revising the Extended Code and including the new Sounds-Write list of the most frequent 3,000 words in English sorted by unit. This would be combined with using the knowledge gained from the Sounds-Write 'Teaching vocabulary in Year 3 to Year 6' courses. We intend to have a revised Year 3 to Year 6 spelling scope and sequence and a bank of lessons ready for implementation for the start of the 2022 school year.

4.　Evaluation

We have evaluated the program by looking at data from standardized tests such as the Year 1 phonics screening and the whole school Young's *Parallel Spelling Tests*[*]. We also looked at PM and Fountas and Pinnell benchmark reading assessments[8] to determine instructional and independent reading levels for fluency and comprehension. Additionally, the Interview Schedule for Students (Daffern & Critten, 2019[9]) (see Table 1) was completed in 2021 to assist in the evaluation of the impact of Sounds-Write across Year 2 to Year 6.

---

8. PM and Fountas and Pinnell benchmark assessments determine students' independent and instructional reading levels. In using these one-on-one assessments, teachers are able to observe and quantify student reading behaviors, engage students in comprehension conversations that go beyond retelling, monitor a student's reading fluency, and make informed decisions that connect assessment to responsive teaching. These assessments are part of a suite of assessments used by teachers to support the reading development of all students.

9. Daffern, T. & Critten, S. (2019). Student and teacher perspectives on spelling. *Australian Journal of Language and Literacy, 42*(1), 40-57

Table 1. Spelling interview questions (Daffern & Critten, 2019, p. 56)

Key questions	Possible probes
When you write a word, but are not sure how to spell it, what do you do?	• What if this happens in a spelling test/when writing a story/some other piece of writing? • What if you cannot use a dictionary, or you cannot ask someone, or you cannot use the computer spell-check? • What do you do with words that you can spell easily?
Can you give me some tips, ideas, or strategies that may help someone become better at spelling?	• What kinds of strategies does your teacher show you in class?
I am going to ask you to write a word/ few words/sentence. As you write, think about how you are spelling each word. Write the word ___, and think aloud while you write.	• What goes through your mind when you write the word ___. • What other kinds of words might you use for this strategy (for example, 'sounding out')? Can you give me some examples?
Here is a word (display a word that the student either correctly or incorrectly wrote). Tell me as much as you can about the spelling of this word?	• Are there any interesting features that you notice about the word and the letters in it? • Do you think this word is correctly spelled? How do you know if the word is correct/incorrect?
What do you find easy/hard about spelling? Why?	• Can you give me some examples of when spelling is easy/hard?

The spelling interviews were carried out with a third of each cohort from Year 2 to Year 6 to ascertain which strategies students were using to spell difficult or unfamiliar words. The spelling interviews demonstrated that students in Year 2 use the strategies they have learned from Sounds-Write to segment, blend, and divide words into syllables, whereas students in the older years relied on memorizing or guessing words. The knowledge that Year 2 students had gained, including the understanding of the schwas, has had a significant impact on their ability to spell unknown words. These students started the Sounds-Write program at the start of Kindergarten in 2019. Conversely, students in Year 3 to Year 6 were able to segment and blend to some extent, however, they were still

Chapter 1

relying on memorizing words and less effective strategies, such as silent letters, bossy 'e', and spelling rules and exceptions. These students have had varying exposure to Sounds-Write as it has been implemented across the school.

For example, when asked "When you write a word but are not sure how to spell it, what do you do?", these were some of the answers Year 2 students gave.

> "Break it up into sounds and syllables."
> "Sound it out, break it up, put it back together."
> "Spellings can have a different sound, like c and s."

The answers given by students in Year 5 were very different.

> "Write it then experiment by adding letters or taking them away."
> "Just have a guess."
> "Sometimes I highlight it to come baåck to it and hopefully it comes into my head later."

When spelling the word 'cattle', Year 2 students made the following observations.

> "I wondered what spelling of /l/ it would be: 'el' or 'le'… 'le' looks right."
> "I wondered if it is a 'tt' or 't'… I remembered it was tt."
> "I said the sounds as I wrote the word. I think it's tt."
> "I think it has an 'e' in there for the 'ugh' (schwa) sound. It is an ll not an l."

When spelling 'favourite', Year 6 students commented.

> "I memorize words to spell them."
> "I remember 'our' is in the middle."
> "I try different spellings and write it down."

The Young's *Parallel Spelling Tests* results from December 2020 show that 93% of students in Kindergarten and Year 1, who have received consistent Sounds-

Write teaching from the start of their schooling in Kindergarten, are spelling at or above chronological age (see Table 2). This is significantly higher than the percentage of students in Year 2 to Year 5 who are spelling at or above their chronological age (77% to 87%). These students in Year 2 to Year 5 have not been explicitly taught Sounds-Write from the beginning of their schooling. Indeed, in these older years, the percentage of students whose spelling ages are more than 6 months below their chronological age is substantially higher, ranging from 9% to 17%.

Table 2. Whole school Young's *Parallel Spelling Tests* assessment data – December 2020

	Kindergarten 57 students		Year 1 58 students		Year 2 87 students		Year 3 62 students		Year 4 88 students		Year 5 64 students	
At or above chronological age	53	93%	54	93%	67	77%	54	87%	69	78%	54	85%
<6 months below	3	5%	3	5%	6	7%	2	3%	4	5%	4	6%
>6 months below	1	2%	1	2%	14	16%	6	10%	15	17%	6	9%

The Year 1 Phonics Screening Check[10] results (Table 3) showed that 85% of students were on track, 12% (seven students) needed monitoring and 3% (two students) needed intervention. These nine students had already been identified through school-based assessments and had received or were receiving learning support.

---

10. The Year 1 Phonics Screening is a New South Wales Department of Education assessment implemented across the Year 1 classrooms in all public schools. The purpose of the assessment is to monitor students who may need additional support in their acquisition of their phonics knowledge. The format and the reporting of the assessment is determined by the Department of Education.

Chapter 1

Table 3. Year 1 Phonics Screening Check results

Phonics proficiency	Number of students	% of students
	58	
on track	49	85%
carefully monitor	7	12%
support required	2	3%

Results from PM and Fountas and Pinnell benchmark reading assessments[11] (Table 4) show that 86% of students had exceeded the expected level by the end of 2020 (Year 1 Term 4), but, for the same cohort, the percentage of students exceeding the expected level had climbed to 93% by July 2021 (Year 2 Term 2). The fact that more students exceeded the expected target by mid-Year 2 compared to their performance in Year 1 shows that student achievement in reading comprehension and fluency had grown in this cohort because of their stronger skills in segmenting, blending, and phoneme manipulation developed through continued rigorous Sounds-Write teaching.

Table 4. Year 1 2020 and Year 2 2021 reading comprehension and fluency benchmark assessment data

	Year 1 Term 4 (level 18)	Year 2 Term 2 (level 22)
exceeded expected target	86%	93%
at expected target	6%	1%
below expected target	8%	3%

5. Recommendations

The Sounds-Write training gives teachers an excellent background knowledge in linguistic phonics and a deep understanding of how students learn to read. The course is expertly taught, lessons are modeled, and teachers are given practical

---

11. This is a reading target set for the Northern Sydney Region of the NSW Department of Education and a benchmark level for schools to ascertain the effectiveness of their teaching of reading. This data is not collected by the NSW Department of Education and comparable data can only be evaluated at school level, grade-by-grade.

experience and feedback on teaching different lessons. Our teachers have come away with renewed confidence in teaching students to read, using an evidence-based approach. The consistency of having all teachers trained and using the same program gives a coherent approach to the teaching of reading and spelling from Kindergarten to Year 3. Reading is taught explicitly, and students quickly demonstrate confidence and success in being able to segment and blend taught sounds as they develop reading fluency and comprehension.

Sounds-Write has also been incredibly successful at improving our students' spelling skills. It has had a positive impact on the quality of student writing as students are able to achieve automaticity in spelling and so focus more on the content of their writing.

We understand from evaluating our data the importance of following the program with fidelity and ensuring that all our teachers from Kindergarten to Year 6 are Sounds-Write trained. Regular reviews and the opportunity to undertake refresher training and coaching sessions will support the consistency and quality of the Sounds-Write instruction in every classroom and for every intervention group. Observations, refresher courses, and coaching sessions not only benefit our staff, they also assist our program evaluation and lead to changes identified to enhance the delivery of Sounds-Write across the school.

Using the Sounds-Write program as a part of our Kindergarten to Year 6 literacy support program provides students still acquiring the skills in units taught in the classroom program to revise and consolidate their learning. This small group intervention has made a huge difference to students who are below grade average and who would possibly not be making improvements with their reading and spelling if they were not being explicitly taught using an evidence-based program like Sounds-Write.

Our focus now is to continue this into Year 3 to Year 6 and develop students' phonological, orthographic, and morphological knowledge. Twelve teachers have now trained in the 'Teaching vocabulary in Year 3 to Year 6' course. We are now reviewing our spelling scope and sequence for Year 4 to Year 6 and creating a bank of lessons on teaching spelling from this program supported by the Sounds-Write list of the most frequent 3,000 words in English, sorted by Sounds-Write unit.

Further challenges moving forward include the impact of our second Covid-19 lockdown in 2021, which saw students miss 13 weeks of school. We will need to closely monitor students on their return to school to determine the impact of learning from home and we will use formative and summative assessments to guide the teaching and learning of Sounds-Write in our classrooms and the learning support program. Year 2 students will return to face-to-face teaching in Week 4 of Term 4, meaning they will have completed our learning from home program for thirteen of the 40 weeks of the school year.

2 Angel Oak Academy, London, England

Charlotte MacKechnie[1]

1. Context

Angel Oak Academy is a two-form[*2] entry mainstream primary school in Peckham, South East London. Students are from a wide range of minority ethnic backgrounds; 55% speak English as an Additional Language (EAL), and many enter school at an early stage of learning English. A large majority of students are supported by additional government funding, including 47.2% of 411 students currently on roll qualifying as eligible for free school meals[*] (compared to a national average of 23% across mainstream primary schools in England).

The predecessor school became an academy[*] within the STEP Academy Trust (a charitable trust with schools in areas of high social deprivation) in February 2015. In September 2015, following a recommendation from a STEP trustee, Angel Oak Academy began the process of implementing Sounds-Write.

2. Implementation

Before implementing Sounds-Write, the percentage of students achieving the threshold to pass the Phonics Screening Check[*] (PSC) (82%) was in line with the national average (77%), yet few students were scoring 40/40 on the PSC.

---

1. STEP Academy Trust, Thornton Heath, England; charlotte.mackechnie@stepacademytrust.org; https://orcid.org/0000-0002-1939-1772

2. An explanation for terms followed by an asterisk can be found in the glossary: https://doi.org/10.14705/rpnet.2022.55.1367

How to cite: MacKechnie, C. (2022). Angel Oak Academy, London, England. In A. Beaven, A. Comas-Quinn & N. Hinton (Eds), *Systematic synthetic phonics: case studies from Sounds-Write practitioners* (pp. 23-30). Research-publishing.net. https://doi.org/10.14705/rpnet.2022.55.1356

Chapter 2

Furthermore, too many students left Key Stage* 2 without being able to read (20%) or write (27%) at the expected standard. Phonics teaching did not continue beyond Year 1 regardless of whether the student was a proficient decoder and despite the fact that the PSC only assesses a fraction of the alphabetic code. It was not that phonics was not working – it was that the academy's approach to teaching phonics, and the programme they were using, were not working.

Figure 1. Timeline of Sounds-Write staff training

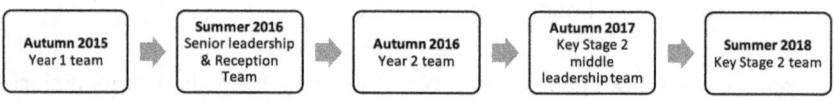

In autumn 2015, the Year 1 team attended the Sounds-Write's 4-day face-to-face course (Figure 1). Using Sounds-Write's Diagnostic Test, the team identified that the majority of the students were not proficient in segmenting, blending, and manipulating words with adjacent consonants. The team, therefore, decided to teach Sounds-Write's Initial Code*, usually taught in Reception, before starting the Extended Code*. Unlike the previous approach, where students were split into attainment groups for phonics lessons, phonics was taught to the whole class with targeted interventions to support students who required additional practice, as recommended by Sounds-Write.

After the first year of implementation, the percentage of students who achieved the threshold to pass the PSC (79%) was still above the national average (74%). However, it was the notable improvement in students' spelling, particularly of polysyllabic words, reported by the Year 1 teachers, which suggested that Sounds-Write was working. The school, therefore, decided to scale-up implementation by implementing Sounds-Write in Reception and Year 2.

At the same time, Angel Oak Academy implemented the three-teacher model (see Figure 2). The school uses the majority of its Pupil Premium Grant* (PPG) to run a three-teacher model throughout the school; three teachers are assigned to each two-form entry year group. Students are taught in three groups of 20 for phonics, reading, English, and maths, and in the afternoon, students are split into two groups of 30 and the additional teacher leads interventions. Whole class phonics is taught in Reception and Key Stage 1, and students who require additional support benefit from same day 'keep-up' interventions at a separate time. Teachers also lead targeted 'catch-up' interventions for students with gaps in their phonemic awareness skills or code knowledge.

Figure 2. Three-teacher model

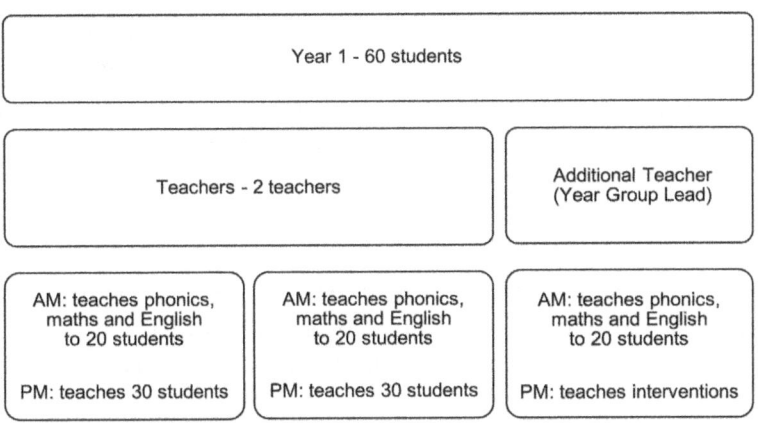

By summer 2017, data from academy-wide assessments showed that students in Key Stage 1 were achieving higher scores on decoding (word-recognition) assessments than students in Key Stage 2. The senior leadership team, therefore, agreed to trial teaching Sounds-Write in Years 3-6, where it was taught to the whole class for 30 minutes, three times per week. Much like in Reception and Key Stage 1, students who required further practice were supported by the additional teacher in the afternoons, attending either 'keep-up' or 'catch-up' interventions, alongside whole class lessons. This meant that by September 2018, all students in Key Stage 2 had worked through the Extended Code. The Key Stage 2 team, therefore, turned their attention to teaching the National Curriculum spelling objectives using the Sounds-Write language, methods, and

Chapter 2

lessons. The teachers planned from centrally-adapted documents provided by the phonics lead[3], based on the National Curriculum, which either categorised words by alternative spellings, alternative pronunciations, or by morpheme.

Today, Sounds-Write is fully implemented across the academy; it is taught daily in Reception and Key Stage 1, and three times a week in Key Stage 2. Sounds-Write's Initial Code is taught in Reception, and the majority of students achieve a good level of development at the end of Reception and enter Year 1 secure in their segmenting, blending, and manipulating skills. Sounds-Write's Extended Code is taught across Key Stage 1, alongside the morphemes from the National Curriculum spelling objectives for Years 1 and 2. In Year 3, students revisit the Extended Code at the polysyllabic level, before beginning the National Curriculum spelling objectives. In Years 4 and 5, students continue to work through the objectives, and in Year 6, students revise spelling objectives or analyse spellings in homophones.

The academy continues to use the majority of its Pupil Premium Grant to run a three-teacher model, so students in every year group are able to access 'keep-up' or 'catch-up' interventions where necessary, and new starters are supported in making rapid progress through one-to-one or small-group interventions.

3. Evaluation

Since implementing Sounds-Write across the academy, student attainment has risen in the Year 1 PSC. Since 2018, the vast majority of students in Year 1 (80-87%) have scored 40/40 on the PSC (Table 1). The students who are not ready to pass the PSC continue to be supported by daily targeted intervention teaching until they achieve the threshold – whether that be at the end of Year 2, or in Year 3.

---

3. https://linguisticphonics.wordpress.com/phonics-from-eyfs-y6/

Across the academy, students are assessed in phonemic awareness (Sounds-Write Diagnostic Test[*]), decoding (the Bryant test, 1975), and fluency (Dibels[4]), and students now reach end of Key Stage 2 expectations for reading fluency (127+ words correct per minute and 99% accuracy) much earlier than previous cohorts.

Table 1. Year 1 PSC – children achieving expected standard

2014	2015	2016[a]	2017[b]	2018	2019	2020
72%	82%	79%	89%	92%	92%	95%

[a] The slight dip in results for 2016 may be due to the first term of Year 1 being spent on the Initial Code, which is typically taught in Reception, prior to starting the Extended Code.

[b] Sounds-Write implemented in Year 1 during the 2016-17 academic year.

Table 2 below shows the percentage of students demonstrating decoding mastery before implementing Sounds-Write (2017), compared with the percentage of students demonstrating decoding mastery after one year of Sounds-Write lessons in Key Stage 2. Although spelling is not formally assessed with standardised testing, teachers continuously formatively assess and have anecdotally reported that students are much more confident spellers when compared to previous cohorts.

Table 2. Key Stage 2 – students demonstrating decoding mastery

	Decoding Mastery (The Bryant Test, 1975)	
	Pre 2017 Sounds-Write	2018 after one year of Sounds-Write
KS2 Students	22%	74%
PPG	28%	68%
Non-PPG	18%	78%
EAL	27%	80%
Non-EAL	18%	69%
SEND[*]	6%	41%
Non-SEND	26%	81%

4. Dynamic Indicators of Basic Early Literacy Skills; https://dibels.uoregon.edu/about-dibels

Chapter 2

The data in Table 2 also shows that there was a substantial increase in SEND students who demonstrated decoding mastery after one year of Sounds-Write in Key Stage 2. This is particularly insightful, as too many students in English speaking schools become unnecessary 'instructional casualties', where the method of teaching does not lead to progress. Several students who had not mastered decoding via the previous phonics approach were able to do so after one year of whole class and intervention Sounds-Write lessons. All students continue to receive targeted intervention teaching until they demonstrate decoding mastery.

Interestingly, EAL students appear to have made more progress than their non-EAL peers. Further research would be required to understand this, and there may be a number of different factors at play, but one possible hypothesis is that some EAL students' progress may be due to the stress and rhythm of their first language, which may match the English orthography more closely than the natural stress and rhythm of first-language English speakers. For example, some EAL students may pronounce English words with fewer *schwas* which is advantageous in spelling, and sometimes explains why students mispronounce words (e.g. pronouncing 'mountain' with emphasis on both syllables, unlike the first-language English speaker's pronunciation of '**moun**tain' with < ai > pronounced as /i/).

When inspected by Ofsted* in 2017, Angel Oak Academy was rated 'Outstanding' and the report deemed that "[a]ttainment in phonics is above average and rising. Pupils also make fast progress in developing wider reading skills. Many can interrogate texts and so gain deep meaning from what they are reading".

However, there is still work to be done. The academy is aware that they must continue to develop their support for students who are eligible for Pupil Premium Grant, as the increase in decoding mastery for those who are non-PPG is much more substantial than those who are eligible for PPG. This is an ongoing priority for not only the academy but for all schools in the multi-academy trust.

Throughout the Covid-19 pandemic, teachers recorded mini-phonics lessons and set independent tasks to support students who were continuing their learning at home. The academy made the decision to focus these Sounds-Write lessons on reviewing previously taught content to support retention, and when students returned to their classrooms, the team were confident that most students had retained most of the knowledge and skills that had been taught prior to partial and wider school closures. However, this has left the academy in a position where, at the beginning of the 2021-22 academic year, students were working approximately five to six months behind where previous cohorts would have been working in each school year. The academy will continue to teach Sounds-Write, as per its systematic structure, and continues to work towards supporting all students in mastering decoding and leaving primary school being able to read and spell fluently.

4. Recommendations

Angel Oak Academy has supported several other academies within STEP Academy Trust in implementing a whole school approach to teaching reading and spelling through Sounds-Write. The academy is one of the UK based Sounds-Write training schools, where open-mornings are hosted and support is provided to external schools.

Much of the advice and recommendations that the staff at Angel Oak Academy share with colleagues at other schools is based on either the successes or challenges they have experienced when implementing and developing their approach to using Sounds-Write for whole class and intervention teaching.

One major challenge was being able to release several members of staff to complete the 4-day face-to-face course. This meant that for one day per week, several members of staff would be off-site for their training. However, the new Sounds-Write Practitioners Online Training (SWPOT) course means that more practitioners can access the training at the same time; as the online course is asynchronous and leaders are able to release staff at different times and on different days across the week.

Chapter 2

The key recommendations from Angel Oak Academy, based on their experience in implementing Sounds-Write, are as follows.

- Teach the programme with fidelity.

- Train all practitioners who are involved with the teaching of reading and writing.

- If budget allows, supplement the programme with matched decodable books (available at Sounds-Write or Phonic Books). If budget does not allow, then access the free, downloadable decodable texts, produced by Sounds-Write (made available to all Sounds-Write practitioners).

- The earlier you intervene with 'keep-up' interventions, the less likely the need for 'catch-up' interventions in the future.

- Support parents and carers by encouraging them to complete the free Sounds-Write course for parents and carers, and by hosting regular open-mornings and workshops in school.

- Invest in the professional development of your phonics coordinator, so that you have an in-house expert who can lead regular continuous professional development. You may also consider enrolling your phonics coordinator on some of the Sounds-Write masterclasses that have recently been introduced.

3 Bloomfield Learning Centre, London, England

Sarah Horner[1] and Jane Orr[2]

1. Context

The Bloomfield Learning Centre (BLC) is a specialist literacy clinic, in Southwark, London. It provides diagnostic assessments and one-to-one teaching for children, aged from seven years to young adults, who are failing at school or unable to partake in further education, due to their inability to read and write fluently. The BLC teaches 84 students per week.

The BLC works primarily with students from socially deprived inner London boroughs. Their parents lack the funds to pay for tutoring and their schools struggle to provide the one-to-one teaching they need. These young people are thus deprived of educational opportunities. At the time of writing, 3.75% of students speak English as a second language.

The BLC is a charity, with no statutory funding. All Sounds-Write lessons are subsidised and 15% of students have full bursaries. Some schools and some parents contribute towards the cost of lessons. The BLC is reliant on donations to cover the budget shortfall.

Students are referred to the BLC primarily by schools or parents, but occasionally by other professionals. During the Covid-19 pandemic, whilst schools were open only to the children of key workers, the usual ratio of school (65%) and parent

---

1. The Bloomfield Learning Centre, London, England; slhorner@hotmail.com

2. The Bloomfield Learning Centre, London, England; janeaorr@gmail.com

How to cite: Horner, S., & Orr, J. (2022). Bloomfield Learning Centre, London, England. In A. Beaven, A. Comas-Quinn & N. Hinton (Eds), *Systematic synthetic phonics: case studies from Sounds-Write practitioners* (pp. 31-41). Research-publishing.net. https://doi.org/10.14705/rpnet.2022.55.1357

(35%) referrals changed dramatically. Between June 2020 and July 2021, 6% of students were referred by schools and 94% by parents.

On referral to the clinic, students are between two and five years behind in reading and spelling. Through the provision of high-quality teaching, the BLC aims to give them all the opportunity to achieve their academic potential and thus leave school with fluent literacy skills and exam success. The Sounds-Write programme is an essential part of this process. Between September 2018 and July 2019, the average increase in reading age of BLC students was 19.1 months.

2. Implementation

All teachers have Level 7 certification[3] in assessing and teaching students with specific learning difficulties, which is considered the highest qualification in this field. Additionally, all teachers are qualified Sounds-Write practitioners. Following the launch of the Sounds-Write programme, the first BLC teacher trained in 2005, followed by the rest of the team between 2006-2008, with new staff training as they joined the team. The Sounds-Write programme is central to our teaching programmes, and is used across all age groups as an intervention strategy.

All BLC teaching is delivered one-to-one, generally for one hour per week. Prior to the pandemic, all lessons were face-to-face, either in the clinic or in schools. During the pandemic, when schools were closed, this model changed. The BLC transferred all teaching online, setting up an online literacy clinic serving students in their homes or, for the children of key workers, in school. Since that time, the BLC has provided both in person and online teaching.

We assess all students referred in order to compile a clear picture of their learning strengths and weaknesses and an individual cognitive profile. This is followed up with a comprehensive written report. Given that all those referred

---

3. A Level 7 certificate indicates study at Master's level, although it may not be equivalent to a Master's.

to the clinic are struggling with literacy, the primary focus of the assessment is to identify the reason for their struggles. Where appropriate, the assessor will make a diagnosis of dyslexia. The main purpose of the report is to inform teaching and make learning as easy, efficient, and fun as possible. Diagnostic assessments for specific learning difficulties/dyslexia investigate the following areas.

- Background information relating to the child's early developmental history including difficulties at birth, the development of spoken language, and fine and gross motor skills. Any difficulties with hearing and eyesight are also recorded.

This is accompanied by questionnaires completed by the parent and class teacher describing the child's school experience – strengths and weaknesses, acquired skills, learning strategies, motivation, and level of enjoyment.

- General underlying ability (verbal and non-verbal) assessed using the WRIT III (Wide Range Intelligence Test III[4]).

- Literacy attainment i.e. reading accuracy, comprehension, speed and fluency, spelling, and writing proficiency.

- Underlying cognitive skills known to be associated with the acquisition of literacy such as auditory short term and working memory, phonological processing (the ability to process the sounds of one's language) and visual processing speed.

3. Evaluation

In order to demonstrate the impact of using Sounds-Write as a programme of intervention, we are presenting an individual case study: Terry.

---

[4]. https://www.pearsonclinical.co.uk/store/ukassessments/en/wide-range/Wide-Range-Intelligence-Test/p/P100009122.html

Chapter 3

3.1. Social and educational background

At the time of writing, Terry (a pseudonym) was in Year 8. He was referred to BLC, by his primary school, when he was in Year 6.

Terry lives in London with his parents and his brother. The family's first language is English. There is a family history of literacy difficulties. Terry reached his early developmental milestones with no physical or developmental issues noted until he entered school in Reception, aged four years. Terry's mother recalls that during his early years of learning, he struggled "with his phonics" and demonstrated poor handwriting skills; he wrote slowly and struggled with pencil control.

Terry's primary school was of average size with 317 students. It is in a deprived part of London, with 41.8% of children receiving free school meals*[5] (national average: 20.8%), and 60.3% of students did not speak English as their first language (national average: 21.2%).

In September 2020, Terry progressed to a mainstream non-selective secondary school, also in London. Here the percentage of free school meals is 28.8% (national average: 19.3%), and 46% of students achieved Grade 5 or above in English and Maths GCSE[6] compared to a national average of 43%.

At school, Terry struggled with initial phonics instruction and found learning to read challenging. School provided small group literacy support up to Year 3, but Terry made limited progress.

Whilst in Year 4, school referred Terry to the Child and Adolescent Mental Health Services for emotional and behavioural issues. This was due to angry and frustrated behaviour that included banging his head against the wall and

---

5. An explanation for terms followed by an asterisk can be found in the glossary: https://doi.org/10.14705/rpnet.2022.55.1367

6. General Certificate of Secondary Education in England, Wales and Northern Ireland.

throwing things in class. Despite a strong, supportive relationship with his mother, it was clear that Terry was a very unhappy child.

This was followed up in July 2017 with an assessment by the Local Education Authority[7] Specific Learning Difficulties team. Although Terry was found to have a strong dyslexic profile, he was not given a diagnosis because of his 'emotional responses'. Therapeutic intervention was suggested, with a recommendation to reassess his educational skills in one year.

3.2. Diagnostic assessment

One year later, in autumn 2019, Terry's school referred him to the BLC for a diagnostic assessment. This took place when he was ten years and nine months old.

Much of the relevant background information for Terry has already been mentioned, but what became immediately apparent during this initial visit to the BLC was his strong dislike of academic work and an absolute sense of failure, which had led to low self-esteem, significant anxiety, and a dislike of school. He was acutely aware of his failure to learn to read.

Assessment reports and yearly reassessments use the convention of standardised scores in order to measure progress; these are briefly explained below.

In order to calculate a standardised score, the raw score is converted to enable comparison of the individual's performance with others of the same chronological age. Standardised scores have a mean of 100, with an average range of 85-115. If a standardised score remains the same over time, this means that the student is making normal progress. If a standardised score increases, this means that the student has made more than normal progress. The following descriptors are used for standardised scores (see Table 1).

---

[7]. Local education authorities (LEAs) in England and Wales were responsible for education within their jurisdictions, but have been progressively phased out and their responsibilities moved to local authorities.

Table 1. Descriptors used for standardised scores

Standardised score	Descriptor
131 or more	Well above average
116-130	Above average
111-115	High average
90-110	Mid average
85-89	Low average
70-84	Below average
69 or less	Well below average

The results of the assessment showed that Terry's non-verbal and verbal underlying ability were in the mid average range, showing him to have average academic potential.

In contrast, Terry's literacy scores, assessed using Weschler Individual Achievement Test 3 (WIAT-3[8]), were strikingly low, showing him to be more than four years behind in reading and spelling. He displayed particular anxiety when asked to write and needed much encouragement before putting pencil to paper. The overall appearance of his writing was immature as he used print rather than cursive script and the speed at which he wrote was well below average (see summary Table 2 below for scores).

Further tests showed that Terry had weaknesses in all areas of phonological processing. He struggled to segment and blend phonemes (speech sounds), performing at the well below average level in both of these areas (Comprehensive Test of Phonological Processing 2 – CTOPP-2[9]).

Terry was given a diagnosis of dyslexia/specific learning difficulty. With transition to secondary school approaching in less than a year, he was immediately identified as a vulnerable student in need of urgent support. This

---

8. https://www.pearsonclinical.co.uk/store/ukassessments/en/Store/Professional-Assessments/Academic-Learning/Reading/Wechsler-Individual-Achievement-Test---Third-UK-Edition/p/P100009274.html

9. https://www.pearsonclinical.co.uk/store/ukassessments/en/Store/Professional-Assessments/Cognition-%26-Neuro/Memory/Comprehensive-Test-of-Phonological-Processing-%7C-Second-Edition/p/P100009101.html

is a challenging time for any child; it was obvious that Terry would be unable to cope.

Terry was offered a full bursary at BLC, starting in January 2020. This comprised one-to-one teaching for one hour per week.

3.3. BLC teaching

Based upon the diagnostic assessment, Terry began the Sounds-Write Programme at Unit 6 of the Initial Code*. Given his weakness in phonological processing, the initial focus was on improving the skills required for reading and writing: segmenting, blending, and manipulating phonemes. Terry initially read decodable books at a level that matched his level of skill/ability. This enabled him to practise these vital skills at the text level and engage his interest in the process of reading, thus increasing his confidence.

A typical session involves a range of Sounds-Write lessons, often followed by a game to reinforce the lesson's target/s. Also included would be passage reading from a decodable book, with attention paid not only to accurate decoding, but also vocabulary development and comprehension. Language development has also been a focus in lessons and continues to include oral work in which Terry is encouraged to incorporate new vocabulary.

After six months of tuition, his mother emailed the centre to say,

> "Terry has come so far and doing so well since he has been coming to the Bloomfield and I'm really happy how well he is doing. Thank you so much for all what you have done with Terry and how you have made him come out of himself and more confidence he has in himself now" (July 2020).

Terry started secondary school in September 2020, in more difficult circumstances than anyone could have predicted, during the pandemic. At the time of writing, he has just started Year 8. Not only is he coping, he is actually enjoying a

Chapter 3

wide range of subjects. When asked which subjects he likes best at school, he responded, "History, Geography, loads of them!".

Terry approaches his Sounds-Write lessons at BLC with enthusiasm. He reads with expression, demonstrating good comprehension of the text. When faced with a word he does not recognise, he makes confident use of his segmenting and blending skills, without prompting, and is able to self-correct. At Terry's final BLC lesson of the academic year he was wearing a badge on his blazer awarded to him for achieving 150 'learning points'.

In July 2021, Terry's mother wrote,

> "Terry didn't get much help in his primary school, that is why Terry needed so much help, I told the school so many time that he is really behind for his age. When Terry was in Year 5 that's when the school seemed to see how much help he did need, which I was not happy with as it took them that long, they just classed him as naughty child but since he has been coming to Bloomfield I can see the change in Terry a lot and I'm really happy and so grateful for all the help you have giving to him and how far he has come along".

Terry was reassessed in June 2021 using the WIAT-3, when he was twelve years and four months old; one year and seven months on from his initial assessment.

Table 2. Standardised scores and age equivalents

	November 2019		June 2021		
	Standardised score	Age equivalent	Standardised score	Age equivalent	Total gain
Single Word Reading	60	6 years	70	7 years 8 months	1 year 8 months
Single Word Spelling	58	5 years 8 months	69	7 years 4 months	1 year 6 months
Reading Comprehension	62	6 years			

It is BLC policy to reassess all students' reading attainment and spelling annually. More specific reassessment relating to phonological skills is carried out when considered appropriate in order to inform teaching. This was challenging during the pandemic whilst teaching was online, which also explains why reading comprehension was not reassessed. Standardised scores and age equivalents are displayed in Table 2 above.

3.4. Summary of main results

Terry attended 67 one hour sessions, during school term times, between January 2020 and June 2021. He has made great progress in reading and spelling, but his literacy skills remain below average for his peer group.

Terry's continued attendance at the BLC is testament to his improved motivation, self-image, and resilience. He is now able to cope in school, is making progress across the curriculum, and sees himself as a learner with academic potential. Terry is optimistic about life after school. He currently aspires to work in the film industry either making films or acting.

4. Recommendations

The following recommendations are ideals, or best practice.

- Students with complex needs benefit from one-to-one teaching focussed on their individual needs.

- Start with a thorough diagnostic assessment to establish a starting point in the Sounds-Write programme.

- Students benefit from a variety of short, well-paced activities within each session; use both the Sounds-Write lessons and appropriate games and activities to reinforce learning.

- Provide homework for students to reinforce current areas of learning between Sounds-Write lessons. This would depend on each student, but may include a variety of activities to support the development of skills and code knowledge, such as those in the Sounds-Write or Phonic Books workbooks, or simple card games that encourage practice.

- Regularly reassess in order to monitor progress.

- Cultivate good communication with parents/carers and schools. This includes communicating programmes of work and targets set, and inviting parents and/or teaching assistants to observe Sounds-Write lessons, enabling them to support students through the week by using accurate language and activities.

- Invest in a range of decodable books that sit alongside the Sounds-Write Programme. Send a weekly reading book home.

- Where possible, work as a team, using a variety of means of communication. Develop a way, such as Google Drive, to create a library of shared resources.

- Access continuous professional development provided by Sounds-Write.

These are some challenges faced by the BLC team.

- Communication with schools can be difficult, especially when students have been referred by their parents.

- Parents with poor literacy can find it very difficult to support their children at home.

- Children often come to the clinic having been taught very different ways of thinking about how reading and spelling work. For example, they may have been taught to think about spelling in terms of letter names, or have imprecise pronunciation of sounds. This inevitably necessitates a certain amount of unlearning before they can truly make progress.

Despite these challenges, we work hard to implement the best practice recommended. As our annual average increases in reading age and Terry's improvement show, one hour per week undoubtedly has a positive impact.

4 Docklands Primary School, Melbourne, Australia

Emina McLean[1]

1. Context

Our brand-new school, Docklands Primary School, opened in January 2021. Located in the heart of Melbourne, Australia, we are a state school for students in Foundation*[2] through to Year 6. At the time of this case study first being written, we had 255 students enrolled, but numbers continue to grow. We have a vibrant and diverse student community, with over 60% of our students speaking English as an additional language. Our students were born in 21 different countries, and there are at least thirteen different languages spoken at home.

As the English and Literacy Leader, I oversee curriculum, assessment, instruction, intervention, and professional learning in those domains. Part of that foundational work has involved ensuring staff are formally trained in Sounds-Write, and that the programme is implemented with consistency and fidelity across classrooms. We teach Sounds-Write in the first three years of school (Foundation-Year 2). Students receive 30 minutes of instruction daily and planning and delivery is consistent across year level classrooms. In 2021, there were six Foundation classes, two Year 1 classes, and one Year 2 class.

We are not considered a particularly advantaged or disadvantaged school, with an Index of Community Socio-Educational Advantage* value close to the average of 1,000 (range of 800-1,200).

---

1. Docklands Primary School, Melbourne, Australia; emina.mclean@gmail.com; https://orcid.org/0000-0002-8199-8495

2. An explanation for terms followed by an asterisk can be found in the glossary: https://doi.org/10.14705/rpnet.2022.55.1367

How to cite: McLean E. (2022). Docklands Primary School, Melbourne, Australia. In A. Beaven, A. Comas-Quinn & N. Hinton (Eds), *Systematic synthetic phonics: case studies from Sounds-Write practitioners* (pp. 43-53). Research-publishing.net. https://doi.org/10.14705/rpnet.2022.55.1358

Chapter 4

2. Implementation

Given we are a brand-new school, Sounds-Write was only implemented in 2021. All teachers in Foundation-Year 2 (n=9) have completed the online training. Most teachers in the upper years and our education support/specialist staff have been trained too. The school Principal and Assistant Principal completed the face-to-face and online training respectively, prior to the school opening, and the English and Literacy Leader completed face-to-face training approximately two years prior to the school opening.

Sounds-Write is delivered as whole-class face-to-face instruction for 30-minutes every morning in Foundation-Year 2 classrooms. In addition, reading practice is provided via reading fluency lessons using decodable sentences and decodable readers, and dictation of words and sentences. Students also take home decodable readers (to read to parents/carers) along with a broad range of children's literature (for parents/carers to read-aloud or with the children), for further reading practice.

Given we had four lockdowns in 2021 due to the Covid-19 pandemic, we had to provide online instruction during those periods. To do this, we used the Sounds-Write digital teaching resources and developed our own teaching materials (e.g. PowerPoint slides). The total amount of instruction per week online was less, reduced to more like 90 minutes per week compared to the usual 150 minutes per week. Online instruction was live whole-class instruction via Webex, with additional one-on-one reading practice with decodable readers whenever possible. Students were also assigned decodable readers via an e-Library. It should be noted that it was not possible for all students to join all online Sounds-Write lessons.

In 2021, Sounds-Write was used for whole-class Tier* 1 instruction, as per the Response to Intervention framework, but it was also used as top-up/ supplementary instruction within classrooms in small groups when possible. It was also used as our Tier 2 intervention for students who do not achieve benchmark scores on word-level reading and spelling assessments in Foundation-Year 2.

For context, the Response to Intervention framework is "a practice of providing high-quality instruction and interventions matched to student need, monitoring progress frequently to make decisions about changes in instruction or goals, and applying [student] response data to important educational decisions" (Batsche et al, 2005, p. 3)[3]. The primary goal is improved outcomes for all students, while the secondary goal is to identify learning difficulties or disabilities in a timely manner. It is a research-based instructional framework that provides "progressively intense instruction" (Hughes & Dexter, 2011, p. 4)[4] based on student need. Tier 1 involves delivering high quality curriculum and using evidence-informed instructional methods. Tier 2 intervention involves small group instruction, and these interventions are considered to be an increased dose of Tier 1 instruction.

This case study is reporting on all students in Foundation-Year 2, aged five to eight years. In total, this is nine separate classes. These students were taught using Sounds-Write for four school terms, which is approximately 40 weeks of instruction, or one academic year. In Australia, the school year runs from the end of January through to the end of December. Having said that, instruction was interrupted by four periods of remote learning in 2021, and while we adopted the Sounds-Write programme from the start of the year, many staff did not complete the online training until April. This meant that the degree of teacher expertise and implementation varied across classrooms in Terms 1 and 2 of that year (the first 10-20 weeks of instruction).

As reported above, Sounds-Write was delivered as whole-class instruction for 30 minutes per day, in all nine classrooms. Many students in Years 1 and 2 required additional teaching as it became evident that they had missed aspects

---

3. Batsche, G., Elliott, J., Graden, J. L., Grimes, J., Kovaleski, J. F., Prasse, D., ... & Tilly III, W. D. (2005). *Response to intervention: policy considerations and implementation*. National Association of State Directors of Special Education.

4. Hughes, C. A., & Dexter, D. D. (2011). Response to intervention: a research-based summary. *Theory into practice, 50*(1), 4-11. https://doi.org/10.1080/00405841.2011.534909

of systematic and explicit phonics instruction in their previous schools. Sixteen Year 1 and 2 students received Tier 2 intervention during 2021. Sessions were either two or three 30-minute sessions per week face-to-face, although intervention sessions continued in small groups online via Webex when possible during remote learning periods.

3. Evaluation

Detailed below are the evaluation tools we used to monitor student progress in word-level reading and spelling, and oral reading fluency.

3.1. Dynamic Indicators of Basic Early Literacy Skills (DIBELS*)

It is important to note that students join us and leave us throughout the year, as there is some transience in our school community. This impacts how well we can interpret DIBELS data at single benchmark points for a few reasons: (1) the total number of students in each year level can change significantly between benchmarks, (2) students have varying degrees of instruction between benchmarks based on when they joined our school, and (3) even if cohort numbers remain relatively stable, the students included in those total numbers are not necessarily all the same students.

Data are therefore reported firstly as total students assessed at each benchmark (Table 1, Table 3, and Table 5), then only students who completed all three benchmarks across the year/completed the full academic year at our school, which is obviously a smaller sample (Table 2, Table 4, and Table 6).

It is also important to note that the second dataset (Table 2, Table 4, and Table 6), which reports on data obtained only from students who completed all three benchmarks and/or were part of the student cohorts for the complete academic year, is a better reflection of instructional impact over time than the first dataset (Table 1, Table 3, and Table 5), which reports on total students assessed.

Table 1. Total students assessed – Foundation (five to six year-olds): students at or above benchmark

Foundation	Nonsense word fluency – correct letter sounds (measured as number of sounds read correctly in one minute)	Nonsense word fluency – words read correctly (measured as number of two to six sound words read correctly in one minute)
March (n=97) After one month of instruction	65% (63)	36% (35)
June (n=112) After five months of instruction	71% (79)	84% (94)
November (n=108) After ten months of instruction	75% (81)	83% (90)

Table 2. Students who completed all benchmarks – Foundation (five to six year-olds): students at or above benchmark

Foundation	Nonsense word fluency – correct letter sounds (measured as number of sounds read correctly in one minute)	Nonsense word fluency – words read correctly (measured as number of two to six sound words read correctly in one minute)
March (n=89) After one month of instruction	63% (56)	35% (31)
June (n=89) After five months of instruction	74% (66)	88% (78)
November (n=89) After ten months of instruction	83% (74)	91% (81)

Teaching of Sounds-Write in Foundation commenced in February (just after the start of the school year in January), with all staff except one, who had completed the training prior to the start of the academic year, completing their training between February and April. Implementation and planning were strongly supported and supervised in Foundation classrooms. Table 1 and Table 2 show the

Chapter 4

growth between March and June in Foundation, even with many students joining the cohort during that time. Students maintained or increased expected growth across the year, with the number of students meeting benchmarks by either staying the same or increasing across correct letter sounds and words read correctly.

In Foundation, students who completed all benchmarks (Table 2) progressed significantly from Benchmark 1 (March) to Benchmark 3 (November), with nonsense word reading (correct letter sounds) improving from 63% to 83%, while nonsense word reading (words recoded correctly) improved from 35% to 91%.

Foundation students did not access our Tier 2 intervention programme, as resources were allocated to catching up students in Years 1-6 who had not had systematic and explicit instruction in reading and spelling in their previous schools. From 2022, all staff will commence the school year trained in Sounds-Write, and Foundation students will access Tier 2 early intervention as required throughout the year. We are aiming for 90% of students at or above benchmark at March, June, and November timepoints in 2022. This is a realistic goal, if 2022 is not further interrupted by COVID-19.

Table 3. Total students assessed – Year 1 (six to seven year-olds): students at or above benchmark

Year 1	Nonsense word fluency – correct letter sounds (measured as number of sounds read correctly in one minute)	Nonsense word fluency – words read correctly (measured as number of two to six sound words read correctly in one minute)	Oral reading fluency (measured as words read correctly per minute – passages)
March (n=38) After one month of instruction	79% (30)	79% (30)	71% (27)
June (n=38) After five months of instruction	69% (26)	79% (30)	68% (26)
November (n=43) After ten months of instruction	74% (32)	84% (36)	74% (32)

Table 4. Students who completed all benchmarks – Year 1 (six to seven year-olds): students at or above benchmark

Year 1	Nonsense word fluency – correct letter sounds (measured as number of sounds read correctly in one minute)	Nonsense word fluency – words read correctly (measured as number two to six sound words read correctly in one minute)	Oral reading fluency (measured as words read correctly per minute – passages)
March (n=35) After one month of instruction	80% (28)	80% (28)	77% (27)
June (n=35) After five months of instruction	66% (23)	83% (29)	74% (26)
November (n=35) After ten months of instruction	80% (28)	89% (31)	77% (27)

In Year 1, students were receiving top-up instruction (whole-class and intervention groups) in code knowledge they had missed in their first year of schooling. This impacted the delivery of our scope and sequence*, with respect to content and pace. Despite this, from Benchmark 1 (March) to Benchmark 3 (November), 80% of students who completed all benchmarks (Table 4) remained able to meet the increasing benchmark standard on nonsense word reading (correct letter sounds) and oral reading fluency (words read correctly), and the number of students able to meet the nonsense word reading (words recoded correctly) benchmark increased from 80% to 89%.

Table 5 and Table 6 show the growth in Year 2 between the June and November benchmarks. The teaching of Sounds-Write with fidelity only really commenced from May once the teacher had completed training in April. It is clear how much this teaching has impacted students' learning in the second half of the year. This was despite students joining us with limited English language and prior exposure to systematic and explicit phonics teaching. With five to six months of high quality whole-class instruction (Tier 1) and top-up intervention (Tier 2) support, the majority finished the year at grade level.

Table 5. Total students assessed – Year 2 (seven to eight year-olds): students at or above benchmark

Year 2	Nonsense word fluency – correct letter sounds (measured as number of sounds read correctly in one minute)	Nonsense word fluency – words read correctly (measured as number of two to six sound words read correctly in one minute)	Oral reading fluency (measured as words read correctly per minute – passages)
March (n=14) After zero months of instruction[a]	79% (11)	64% (10)	71% (10)
June (n=20) After zero to one month of instruction[a]	45% (9)	50% (10)	50% (10)
November (n=27) After five to six months of instruction[a]	82% (22)	78% (21)	67% (18)

[a] Teacher completed Sounds-Write training in April.

Table 6. Students who completed all benchmarks – Year 2 (seven to eight year-olds): students at or above benchmark

Year 2	Nonsense word fluency – correct letter sounds (measured as number of sounds read correctly in one minute)	Nonsense word fluency – words read correctly (measured as number of two to six sound words read correctly in one minute)	Oral reading fluency (measured as words read correctly per minute – passages)
March (n=14) After zero months of instruction[b]	79% (11)	64% (9)	71% (10)
June (n=14) After zero to one month of instruction[b]	57% (8)	64% (9)	57% (8)
November (n=14) After five to six months of instruction[b]	100% (14)	86% (12)	71% (10)

[b] Teacher completed Sounds-Write training in April.

In Year 2, students were also receiving top-up instruction (whole-class and intervention groups), although Sounds-Write instruction did not formally commence until May, just before Benchmark 2 (June). From Benchmark 2 (June) to Benchmark 3 (November), students in Year 2 improved significantly across the board (see Table 5 and Table 6). On the nonsense word reading (correct letter sounds) subtest, the percentage of students at or above benchmark improved from 57% to 100%. On nonsense word reading (words recoded correctly) and oral reading fluency (words read correctly), the percentages of students at or above benchmark improved from 64% to 86%, and 57% to 71% respectively.

3.2. Year 1 Phonics Screening Check (Australia[5])

Table 7 shows that 69% of our Year 1 students 'passed' the Australian Phonics Check, which means they scored at or above 28/40. These students are considered 'fluent decoders'. Students with a score of 20-27 are considered 'developing decoders', and students with a score of 19 and below are considered 'struggling decoders'. The average score for this cohort was 29.5/40. The Phonics Check currently is only mandated in one state in Australia (South Australia), but this gives us a local comparison. In South Australia, 43% of students passed in 2018, 52% passed in 2019, 63% passed in 2020, and 67% passed in 2021.

Table 7. Year 1 Phonics Screening Check results

Fluent decoders	Developing decoders	Struggling decoders
69%	18%	13%

We expect to see better results next year when our current Foundation cohort who have had Sounds-Write from the start of their first year of school move into Year 1. We expect even better results the following year (2023), when the 2022 Foundation cohort move into Year 1 after optimal instruction with all staff trained from the outset, and hopefully no further remote learning periods.

---

5. https://literacyhub.edu.au/families/the-phonics-check.html

3.3. MOTIf Diagnostic Spelling Tests[6]: spelling of sounds, nonsense words, and irregular words

The assessments shown on Table 8 were conducted in November, following almost a full year of schooling. Foundation and Year 1 cohorts had been taught via Sounds-Write since February (ten months of instruction/intervention), while the Year 2 cohort had been taught via Sounds-Write since May (five to six months of instruction/intervention).

Table 8. MOTIf Diagnostic Spelling Tests (% of students within or above the average range)

	Spelling of Sounds (DiSTs)	Spelling of Nonsense Words	Spelling of Irregular Words
Foundation	83%	59% within or above the average range for Year 1	
Year 1	76%	81%	83%
Year 2		80%	84%

Overall, 81% of our Foundation-Year 2 students are within or above the average range (as per MOTIf test norms) for their grade on spelling measures following their Sounds-Write instruction in 2021. This data is very pleasing, as independent application of knowledge on spelling tasks is perhaps one of the best measures of how effective the instruction has been.

When we collate and average student performances across word-level reading, oral reading fluency and word-level spelling assessments, 80% of our students performed at or above grade level by the end of 2021. We are thrilled with this progress, given the many challenges of starting a new school during a pandemic. We will be analysing longitudinal data to measure our effectiveness over time, once implementation of Sounds-Write is entirely consistent across year levels, and routine for all students from their first year with us. We look forward to improving on our first-year outcomes.

---

6. https://www.motif.org.au/home/tests

4. Recommendations

Training is essential for all staff if Sounds-Write is to be taught well and in a consistent manner. While the training is outstanding and comprehensive, ongoing work to support consistency and fidelity is essential. The job is never 'done'.

What we have done and are doing:

- mapped out teaching of units across Foundation-Year 2 so staff are clear on what will be taught when (detailed scope and sequence);

- team planning via a consistent planning document outlining fortnightly instruction for each year level (i.e. which Sounds-Write lessons and which words/how many words across the ten days in the fortnight);

- modelling, observation, feedback, coaching, and goal setting;

- feedback on planning, pace, amount of content, and script adherence;

- regular leadership team walk-through to observe and provide year level feedback;

- professional learning on assessments which are designed to measure teacher effectiveness and student progress, and establishing clear links between what we are teaching and what we are assessing;

- supporting staff to conduct formative assessment and error correction daily; and

- supporting staff to evaluate assessment data and set goals for student learning.

5 Johnson STEAM Academy Magnet School, Cedar Rapids, Iowa, USA

Katie Eichhorn[1], Kathy Gilbert[2], Myra Hall[3], Gretchen Lawyer[4], and Jill Nunez[5]

1. Context

Johnson Science, Technology, Engineering, Art, and Mathematics (STEAM) Academy Magnet School (JSA) is a Magnet Schools of America Certified with Distinction Demonstration School[6] located in Cedar Rapids, Iowa, in the USA. Embedding STEAM themes across content areas creates an engaging and innovative learning experience for JSA students that positively impacts their future and ignites their passion for learning. As of June 2021, 379 students are enrolled in grades Kindergarten (five years of age) through Grade 5 (ten years of age). The school population is 42% white and 58% non-white, with subgroups of 39% African American, 12% Mixed Race, and 7% Hispanic/Latino. It does not house a program for English language learners, who are served by other schools in the District. JSA has a 20% homelessness rate and a transiency*[7] rate of 25%. Prior to the global pandemic, 77% of JSA students were eligible for Free and

---

1. Johnson STEAM Academy, Cedar Rapids, Iowa, United States; keichhorn@crschools.us

2. Johnson STEAM Academy, Cedar Rapids, Iowa, United States; kgilbert@crschools.us

3. Literacy consultant, Cedar Rapids, Iowa, United States; mhall@gwaea.org

4. Johnson STEAM Academy, Cedar Rapids, Iowa, United States; glawyer@crschools.us

5. Johnson STEAM Academy, Cedar Rapids, Iowa, United States; jnunez@crschools.us

6. At the time of their designation as a Magnet Schools of America Demonstration School, JSA was one of only 13 elementary schools in the USA with that distinction. Magnet Schools of America defines a magnet school as "the single largest form of public school 'choice', magnet schools are visionary, innovative and open to all students regardless of zip code... each school typically focuses on individually themed curricula".

7. An explanation for terms followed by an asterisk can be found in the glossary: https://doi.org/10.14705/rpnet.2022.55.1367

How to cite: Eichhorn, K., Gilbert, K., Hall, M., Lawyer, G., & Nunez, J. (2022). Johnson STEAM Academy Magnet School, Cedar Rapids, Iowa, USA. In A. Beaven, A. Comas-Quinn & N. Hinton (Eds), *Systematic synthetic phonics: case studies from Sounds-Write practitioners* (pp. 55-62). Research-publishing.net. https://doi.org/10.14705/rpnet.2022.55.1359

Chapter 5

Reduced Lunch. However, through the US Government Community Eligibility Program, the entire school population currently receives free breakfast and lunch at school.

The school building and grounds occupy one city block in an older, residential neighborhood known as Wellington Heights. Most students walk or get rides to and from school. Ten percent of the students enroll as lottery students (they apply and are randomly selected) and come from other areas around the city, and bus transportation is provided. In the last five years, schoolwide reading scores have fluctuated between 44% and 55% of students scoring proficient (at grade level) on state accountability measures.

The building that houses JSA has been a neighborhood school for over a century. American poet and novelist Paul Engle grew up in the area and the Paul Engle Association for Community Arts exists today to further his passion for the arts. JSA has an extensive extracurricular after school program as well as before and after school care, and JSA families see the school as a vital stakeholder in their community.

2. Implementation

In spring 2020, the JSA literacy leaders were at a decision point on how to spend available funds to explore effective literacy practices and think 'outside the box' to support student achievement. Funds for literacy efforts had been donated by a local church, and JSA had Every Student Succeeds Act (ESSA, US government) funds to be used on school improvement priorities. Members of the Propel Literacy Forward (Propel) leadership team had been investigating effective literacy instructional practices and had come across John Walker's blog[8] and information about the Sounds-Write synthetic phonics approach. Finding the information promising and in alignment with their professional beliefs, they implemented elements of Walker's approach in first and second grade small

---
8. https://theliteracyblog.com

reading groups with success. Students were engaged and excited when they participated in the Sounds-Write Word Building and Sound Swap routines. Teachers celebrated when students quickly learned and applied the concept that letters are symbols (spellings) that represent sounds. Teachers were intrigued by the concept of teaching sounds in words instead of in isolation. As a result of this practical success, the Propel team voted to invite additional team members as well as interested staff to engage in the summer Sounds-Write training in order to begin instruction by fall of 2020.

In early summer 2020, six JSA teachers, two coaches, and four Grant Wood Area Education Agency support team members took the online Sounds-Write practitioner's training with a UK Trainer. Fourteen more JSA teachers completed the training throughout the 2020/2021 school year and into summer 2021. As a result of this teacher-driven grassroots, organic effort, within one calendar year (during the once-in-a-century pandemic), 75% of the JSA certified staff that teach reading became Sounds-Write practitioners. Teacher buy-in was immediate and robust. Enthusiasm and support for Sounds-Write was, and continues to be, extremely high.

At JSA, Sounds-Write is taught whole group, small group, and one-to-one depending on the grade level and student need. Student response to Sounds-Write lessons was immediately positive due to the high level of engagement, reduced cognitive load and rigor of this program. Sounds-Write is taught in Grades 1 and 2, to complement our literacy programming which also includes interactive read alouds and writing practices. Sounds-Write is taught in Grades 3 to 5 as an intervention to accelerate student learning of the alphabetic code, and explicitly teach and practice skills of segmenting, blending, and phoneme manipulation.

3. Evaluation

Data results were very encouraging even though we taught our first year of Sounds-Write during a global pandemic and an unprecedented natural disaster in Iowa (August 2020 Midwest Derecho[9]) which delayed the start of the school year by four weeks.

3.1. First grade text reading proficiency state assessment

In spring 2021, 38% of our first-graders were proficient on the text reading subtest of the State of Iowa assessment, known as Curriculum-Based Measures Reading[10] (CBMR). Prior years' data (2017-2018 and 2018-2019) showed 32% and 33% proficiency, so our team was encouraged by the 5-6% increase in text reading by our first-graders. Despite a month's delay to the start of the 2020/2021 school year due to the August 2020 Midwest Derecho and three weeks of all-school remote learning in November 2020 caused by the global pandemic, our students showed growth on our end-of-year state assessment (Table 1).

Table 1. JSA CBM-Reading spring results

	17-18	18-19	19-20	20-21
Word Segmenting	76%	68%	-	73%
Nonsense Word Reading	52%	52%	-	52%
Sight Words	36%	45%	-	38%
CBMR (one minute read of three short passages)	33%	32%	-	38%

As we dug deeper into the data, we discovered that overall student proficiency on the State of Iowa assessment was higher in classrooms where Sounds-Write was taught the **entire** school year. We tracked first and second grade in-person classrooms where Sounds-Write was taught the entire year versus all classrooms, which included those rooms where Sounds-Write was taught only part of the year (due to the fact that teachers were trained at different times during the year). The greatest improvement was seen in first-graders: 48% of the students in the Sounds-Write classrooms were proficient compared to only 40% of students in all classrooms. In second grade classrooms, the difference was smaller but still

---

9. A derecho is a widespread wall of very strong winds that result in severe thunderstorms, tornadoes, torrential rains, and flash floods; https://en.wikipedia.org/wiki/August_2020_Midwest_derecho?scrlybrkr=65d2fd65

10. https://my.vanderbilt.edu/specialeducationinduction/files/2013/07/IA.Reading-CBM.pdf

showed that Sounds-Write classrooms did better; the Sounds-Write classrooms were 33% proficient versus 32% in all classrooms.

3.2. Individual Education Plan (IEP) and English language learners

Our special education team witnessed multiple successes with their IEP students. For the purpose of this chapter, we selected one student from each grade level (Table 2).

A first-grader grew by 79 Words Per Minute (WPM). The benchmark expected reading growth for first grade is 54 WPM. A second-grader grew by 41 WPM – about the same as the expected growth of 45 WPM. A third-grader and a fourth-grader increased their WPM by 51 words – significantly above the expected growth for those grades of 38 and 32 WPM respectively. A fifth-grader attending virtual school all year grew by 29 WPM, very close to the benchmark of 30 WPM.

Table 2. Reading growth for IEP and English as a second language students

	Johnson STEAM Academy				State of Iowa Expected Reading Growth			
	Fall	Winter	Spring	Growth in WPM	Fall	Winter	Spring	Growth in WPM
1st Grader	9	30	88	+79	12	37	66	+54
2nd Grader	25	43	66	+41	56	84	101	+45
2nd Grader (ELL)	7	17	68	+61				
3rd Grader	85	114	136	+51	87	110	125	+38
4th Grader	48	70	99	+51	115	133	147	+32
5th Grader	44	59	73	+29	132	149	162	+30

Our special education teachers were riveted by these increases, which they had not seen using other phonics programs. They saw increased engagement by students who in the past had often felt defeated when it came to reading. Small successes early in the program propelled these students forward and helped them make significant gains, which teachers believed would not have happened without our Sounds-Write implementation. For example, the fourth-grader who made above-average progress of +51 WPM had only achieved below average progress in previous years before Sounds-Write had been implemented: +19 WPM in the third grade and +5 WPM in the second grade (substantially below expectations of +38 and +45 WPM improvement in third and second grade respectively – see Table 2 above).

Although JSA does not have a program for English language learners, we do have a small number of students whose home language is not English. Teachers were happy to see the exceptional progress made by an ELL second-grader whose reading increased by +61 WPM in one academic year, far exceeding the expectations for second grade students (+45 WPM) (see Table 2 above).

3.3. Middle school students with reading goals (IEP)

Given concern for reading performance challenges observed in Grade 7 students, a middle school classroom teacher reached out to get support from one of the Sounds-Write-trained Grant Wood Area Education Agency support team members. District assessment data suggested that these students were performing up to four years below their current grade level. Initial steps were to collect data using the Sounds-Write Diagnostic Test (to determine code knowledge and segmenting, blending, and phoneme deletion skills) which would be used to design instruction.

Through the partnership, the teacher was willing to try some innovative instructional approaches with the intention of carefully monitoring student growth. The Sounds-Write approach was used in specially designed instruction for one-to-one and small group interventions aimed at eliminating misconceptions of how to sound out words in order to independently and accurately decode unknown words.

Students A and B in Table 3 had not yet learned how to say individual sounds with precision. They were taught to segment words into syllables and individual sounds – we call this using a 'spelling voice'. Of the three seventh-graders shown in Table 3, Student B showed the most significant improvement. District assessment data showed a jump in performance from Grade 3 in fall 2020 to Grade 5 in spring 2021. All students who participated in the Sounds-Write instruction showed growth in segmenting, blending, phoneme deletion, and code knowledge (see Table 3).

Table 3. Sounds-Write Diagnostic Test results – fall 2020 to spring 2021 improvement

	Segmenting			Blending			Sound deletion			Code knowledge		
	Fall	Spring	Change	Fall	Spring	Change	Fall	Spring	Change	Fall	Spring	Change
Student A	75%	91%	+16	86%	100%	+14	70%	80%	+10	58%	96%	+38
Student B	55%	100%	+45	85%	93%	+8	30%	80%	+50	48%	94%	+46
Student C	86%	100%	+14	93%	93%	0	70%	80%	+10	78%	94%	+16

During read-aloud tasks, the classroom teacher observed students deliberately applying the skills, code knowledge, and conceptual understandings that were taught through Sounds-Write, which enabled students to access grade level texts. Sounds-Write lessons were met with high levels of engagement and confidence. As evidenced in this project, Sounds-Write holds promise as an effective intervention to correct misconceptions and phonics skill gaps in older students.

4. Recommendations

Seven key practices helped us be successful in our first year of implementation. We recommend them to future teams who plan to use Sounds-Write in their schools.

- Form a Sounds-Write **leadership team** to meet regularly – preferably weekly – to oversee implementation. This kept our work front and center.

- Establish **communication with district leaders** to get approval to pilot Sounds-Write. We kept our district contacts informed about our work and got permission to proceed with training and implementation.

- Build a **central resource bank**, such as Google Drive, making all resources easily accessible to teachers. In the early months of our implementation, each teacher was building their own resources. By the end of the school year, we realized we would all benefit from one location for resources. We assigned two teachers to approve everything that was added to Google Drive.

- Pay teachers **a stipend to take the Sounds-Write course**. Our Principal felt the course time commitment required an additional benefit to teachers, so she advocated for them to receive a stipend.

- Seek **outside funding to supplement implementation costs** – such as decodable readers. We were fortunate to have the support of a local church who encouraged our 'outside the box' thinking in terms of literacy practices. They gave generously to our school allowing us to buy decodable readers for the Initial Code* and Extended Code*.

- Establish an **assessment plan** using the Sounds-Write Diagnostic Test as a pre-, post-, and common formative assessments for progress monitoring data collection.

- Provide implementation monitoring resources for teachers to **engage in reflection on Sounds-Write practices** as well as peer coaching to ensure integrity to the Sounds-Write lessons and principles.

6. Merllyn Community Primary School, Bagillt, North Wales, United Kingdom

Tracy Jones[1]

1. Context

Ysgol Merllyn (Merllyn Community Primary School) is located in the village of Bagillt in North Wales (UK), an old lead-mining village in a semi-rural location. It is a state primary with 150 students aged three to eleven, of which 26% are entitled to free school meals and 12% have English as an Additional Language (EAL). Transiency is 8% and 12% of students have Additional Learning Needs (ALN), including 8% with behavioral needs.

The school had previously taught the infants*[2] (aged four to seven) using a synthetic phonics programme, however, there were many children coming through the infants who still did not have a secure knowledge of sound-spelling correspondences, and were not able to segment, blend, and manipulate phonemes. Many children in the juniors* required intervention due to poor reading and decoding skills.

2. Implementation

In 2018, our school was in contact with Three Bridges Primary School in Southall, London. We noticed that their children's reading was incredible. Children in the Reception class, aged four and five, were writing in sentences about the story they were learning about. The spelling was mostly accurate, and they were very

---

1. Ysgol Merllyn, Bagillt, Wales, United Kingdom; head@ysgolmerllyn.org

2. An explanation for terms followed by an asterisk can be found in the glossary: https://doi.org/10.14705/rpnet.2022.55.1367

How to cite: Jones, T. (2022). Merllyn Community Primary School, Bagillt, North Wales, United Kingdom. In A. Beaven, A. Comas-Quinn & N. Hinton (Eds), *Systematic synthetic phonics: case studies from Sounds-Write practitioners* (pp. 63-70). Research-publishing.net. https://doi.org/10.14705/rpnet.2022.55.1360

© 2022 Tracy Jones (CC BY)

Chapter 6

confident readers. We noticed that nearly all children were passing the Phonics Screening Check* in Year 1 and enquired about how they were getting such good results. The head explained that they were using Sounds-Write and put us in touch with the team.

Sounds-Write was implemented initially in Reception, Year 1, and Year 2 from September 2018 (see Table 1). The teachers used the Sounds-Write Diagnostic Test to be able to identify the extent to which children knew their sound-spelling correspondences, and could segment, blend, and manipulate phonemes. In the second year of implementation, the Key Stage* 2 teachers and teaching assistants were trained and then assessed the juniors to identify gaps in code knowledge and skills. At this point, we ended any other literacy interventions to maintain fidelity to the programme and moved over to Sounds-Write.

Table 1. Timeline of staff training

May 2018	May 2019	June 2020	2020
Infants teachers 4-day face-to-face training	Infants teaching assistants and KS1 teachers 4-day face-to-face training	Headteacher and all other untrained teachers and teaching assistants online training	Online training for KS2 Years 3-6 programme

As soon as they are appointed, new teachers or teaching assistants are booked onto the next available Sounds-Write training course. Sounds-Write is delivered across the school with additional targeted support when necessary.

During the first Covid-19 lockdown starting March 2020, the teachers made videos of Sounds-Write lessons for the infant children and sent learning packs home. All parents and carers were encouraged to complete the free Sounds-Write Course for parents and carers to enable them to support their children. In Wales, children returned to school in June 2020 and the teachers carried out the diagnostic test to check if children had retained their code knowledge and skills. The data showed that the children had not lost their code knowledge and skills during this time of online teaching. Sounds-Write lessons continued as normal until the second lockdown in January-March 2021. The teachers continued to record video lessons for the children. Children in the juniors who were on targeted support had one-to-one live Sounds-Write lessons daily. The juniors staff produced learning packs for the children to practise their code knowledge and skills. They also developed their word building, reading longer texts, and comprehension linked to a specific novel or story. Overall, there was approximately 80% engagement in home learning.

This case study discusses the tracking information for our current (2021) Year 3 class. They have been taught using Sounds-Write from Reception and have received targeted support and interventions when necessary and there was very good engagement in home learning. There are 20 children in the class. Although it is not a requirement in Wales, we carried out the Phonics Screening Check at the end of Year 1 and 90% of the children achieved a pass. Two children were receiving targeted support before lockdown (one EAL and one with specific difficulties in blending).

3. Evaluation

Once the children have been taught the Initial Code*, they progress onto the Extended Code*. The data in Table 2 and Table 3 shows the progress between November 2020 and September 2021 for the children who are currently in Year 3. These children were in Year 2 when the first part of the test was conducted (Table 2), seven months after the start of the pandemic.

The test evaluated the students' knowledge of sound-spelling correspondences in the Extended Code. The grey highlights in Table 2 show that the children knew what sounds could be represented by these spellings. Note that Student 5 was an EAL student, new to English, Student 18 had struggled to retain any Initial Code knowledge and was receiving additional targeted support, and Student 14 had very poor attendance and had many challenges that impacted on learning.

In March 2020, the school closed for lockdown and the children did not return physically to school until September 2020. Diagnostic tests were carried out to

Chapter 6

identify code knowledge and skills gaps. We then tiered the children depending on their needs and provided timetabled targeted support when necessary.

Although the Extended Code should start in Year 1, due to the lockdown, we did not want to introduce any new sounds until we had the cohort back, so we spent time revising and consolidating sounds and skills already taught.

By November 2020, this cohort had been taught Units 1 to 5 of the Extended Code. This diagnostic test was carried out as we were facing another national lockdown and we wanted to see what code knowledge and skills the children had retained.

Table 2. November 2020 (children in Year 2)

Students	sh	ck	th	ch	nn	er	ea	ay	oa	ai	ou	ee	ow	ir	ey	ie	aw	ew	oo	oi	ue	ui	au	oy	ur
1																									
2																									
3																									
4																									
5																									
6																									
7																									
8																									
9																									
10																									
11																									
12																									
13																									
14																									
15																									
16																									
17																									
18																									
19																									
20																									

The second lockdown in Wales meant the children were learning from home from December 2020 to February 2021. During this lockdown, children receiving targeted support had one-to-one online Sounds-Write lessons, teachers were filming themselves teaching Sounds-Write and sending work home. Student 18 was in our childcare hub[3] and received one-to-one sessions every day. This really helped him develop his code knowledge and skills (see Table 3) and over time he had a lot more confidence and was experiencing success. Student 5 was offered online one-to-one every day and also made very good progress (see Table 3).

The tests were done again early in September 2021 (see Table 3), when the children had returned from the summer holidays and were at the start of Year 3. The notes in the boxes in Table 3 identify sound-letter correspondences that were not secure enough so needed some very short-term intensive intervention.

We attribute the progress made by the children to the pedagogy of Sounds-Write. Even with the continued disruption, the children continued to gain code knowledge and skills, which were now in their long-term memory. The diagnostic tests are designed to show exactly the weaker areas of code knowledge and skills and this ensures that the targeted provision is very specific to what needs more teaching.

The impact of Sounds-Write implementation, despite lockdowns and missed teaching and learning, is clear. Nearly all children entering the juniors are confident, skilled readers, their automatic decoding enables them to orthographically map words and free up working memory to focus on word meaning and comprehension. The disruption in learning has shown minimal impact as they move through the programme. The Year 3 teachers report this is the first year that there is real confidence in reading in a Year 3 cohort and they have good skills during guided reading sessions to decode unfamiliar words quickly.

---

3. Childcare hubs, mostly located in schools, provided critical childcare and education for the children of key workers (health, education, transport, etc.) during those periods of the pandemic when schools moved to online teaching in Wales.

Chapter 6

Table 3. September 2021 (children in Year 3)

Students	sh	ck	th	ch	nn	er	ea	ay	oa	ai	ou	ee	ow	ir	ey	ie	aw	ew	oo	oi	ue	ui	au	oy	ur
1												ee							o						
2																									
3										ow		ow													
4																									
5																									
6																							ay		
7																									
8		f				e	ow																		
9						e																			
10		ch	sh																						
11																									
12																									
13																									
14																									
15																									
16																									
17																									
18																									
19																									
20																									

4. Recommendations

Implementing Sounds-Write in school needs careful planning, and it is necessary to ensure that there is a phonics lead who is absolutely committed to the role and trained on leading phonics. Our Phonics Lead has attended the Sounds-Write Masterclass: Leading Phonics and will regularly check into sessions to ensure staff are keeping to the scripts and there is fidelity to the programme across the school. In addition, our Phonics Lead regularly meets with the practitioners delivering phonics and interventions to discuss practice and progress. She will ensure sounds are said precisely and sound-spelling correspondences are being taught correctly and liaise where necessary with Speech and Language support and EAL support. Before lockdown, she also held sessions for parents and carers to observe lessons in her classroom. In each Sounds-Write session over two weeks, three parents were invited in to watch and take part in the sessions.

The purpose of this was to ensure that if parents and carers wanted to support, they were teaching phoneme to grapheme at the same time and not in isolation. The parents were also encouraged to download the Sounds-Write app for home learning.

Introducing Sounds-Write in Reception is quite straightforward, however, as you move further up the school where the students have not had previous Sounds-Write teaching of the Initial Code, students' code knowledge and skills can be underdeveloped, but you do not necessarily want to start from the beginning. It will take at least a couple of years with older children to get them where they should be. We attempted to overcome this by initially carrying out the Diagnostic Test with all children. They had been taught with a different phonics scheme, but the code knowledge and skills were not embedded into long-term memory and some children were used to guessing. Some children were significantly behind, so in addition to whole-class lessons, they received daily intensive support in order to support their progress.

Although we do not have to use the Phonics Screening Check in Wales, we choose to use it in our school, as it gives us a comparison with England, where phonics teaching and learning is mandatory. In Wales, there is no requirement to use an accredited synthetic phonics scheme. This leaves schools with the autonomy to decide how reading is to be taught. This can be a challenge as children joining from other schools might not have the same code knowledge and skills as their cohort, and may require intensive support to bring them in line with their peers. Additionally, when transitioning to high schools (ages 12-19), children from different primary schools might have been taught different strategies, which may cause issues for the high schools.

Our school has been research-informed for many years and draws on effect sizes and the work of Professor John Hattie and the Visible Learning MetaX

Chapter 6

database[4], which has up-to-date information on worldwide research into strategies with the potential to accelerate learning. To understand the data, 0.4 is one year's growth in learning for one year's input, therefore our school looks to implement and measure the impact of strategies with a higher than 0.4 effect size. Current research shows that phonics instruction has an effect size of 0.57 and phonological awareness has an effect size of 0.75 (for comparison, the effect size of the Whole Language* approach to literacy development is 0.09). This indicates that children can potentially make fast progress by implementing phonics instruction and focusing on phonological awareness, as Sounds-Write does.

This year, as part of the new ALN reforms in Wales, we are providing targeted support for any children across the school who may need additional support to acquire age-appropriate reading skills and knowledge. We are using a response to intervention approach using a tiered system. Children are assessed and placed in Tier* 1, 2, and 3. Children on Tier 2 will receive at least three additional one-to-one or group interventions per week in order for them to be placed back in Tier 1, once they have caught up with their peers. Children in Tier 3 will generally require intense and additional support, in nearly all instances for wellbeing and emotional issues.

We are also planning to provide intensive support to Year 1 children, in addition to daily phonics lessons, who have missed much of their first two years due to Covid. This will include Sounds-Write whole-class lessons and five additional one-to-one or group interventions per week as they move from the Initial Code to the Extended Code until they have caught up. The impact of this additional support will be evaluated in December 2021.

---

4. https://www.visiblelearningmetax.com/

7 Nollamara Primary and Intensive English School, Perth, Australia

Kendall Hammond[1]

1. Context

Nollamara Primary and Intensive English School (NPS) is situated seven kilometers north of the Perth Central Business District in Western Australia. Our Index of Community Socio-Educational Advantage*[2] (ICSEA) is 939[3] and the school caters for students from Kindergarten* to Year 6. There are currently 309 students who are supported by 50 staff.

NPS was opened in 1956 and an Intensive English Center (IEC), supporting newly arrived humanitarian and refugee students, commenced in 2005. The school has a diverse population (see Figure 1), and there are more than 76% of students with a language background other than English at the school, with approximately 45 language groups. The larger groups include Arabic 13%, Dinka 7%, Karen 4.5%, and Burmese, Swahili, Vietnamese, and Kirundi which combined represent 10% of the cohort. Aboriginal students make up 8% of our school community.

There is a high transiency* rate at NPS, approximately 51%. This is due to the students in the IEC returning to their local school after one to two years on

---

1. Nollamara Primary and Intensive English School, Nollamara, Australia; kendall.hammond@education.wa.edu.au

2. An explanation for terms followed by an asterisk can be found in the glossary: https://doi.org/10.14705/rpnet.2022.55.1367

3. "ICSEA values are calculated on a scale which has a median of 1000 and a standard deviation of 100. ICSEA values typically range from approximately 500 (representing schools with extremely disadvantaged student backgrounds) to about 1300 (representing schools with extremely advantaged student backgrounds)" https://www.myschool.edu.au/media/1820/guide-to-understanding-icsea-values.pdf.

How to cite: Hammond, K. (2022). Nollamara Primary and Intensive English School, Perth, Australia. In A. Beaven, A. Comas-Quinn & N. Hinton (Eds), *Systematic synthetic phonics: case studies from Sounds-Write practitioners* (pp. 71-78). Research-publishing.net. https://doi.org/10.14705/rpnet.2022.55.1361

Chapter 7

specialist English language intervention. Many families are in temporary or rental accommodation, which impacts on student enrollment, too.

The school has a full-time chaplain, school psychologist (two and a half days a week), two Aboriginal Islander Education Officers (AIEO), and two multicultural liaison officers who support students and families as well as engage local agencies. The school also provides intervention with trauma counseling, speech therapists, and occupational therapists.

Figure 1. Demographic data[4]

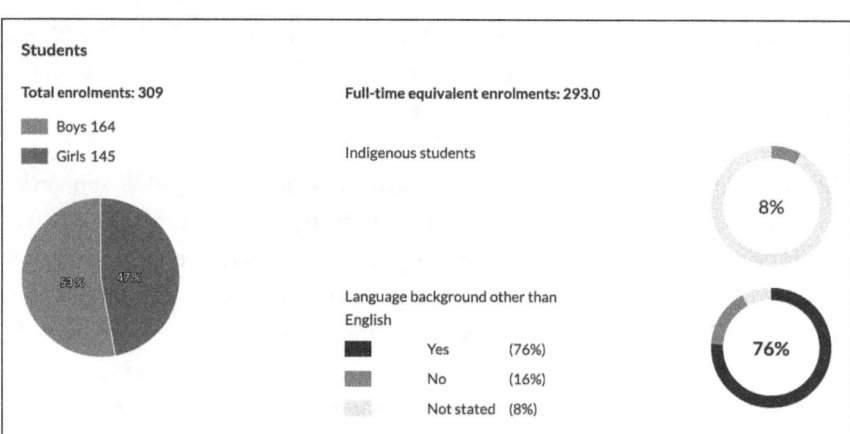

Due to data indicating that the school needed improvement in the areas of literacy and numeracy, the school applied for and was successful in gaining a partnership with the Fogarty Foundation's EDvance program. This is an initiative for school improvement that offers an integrated leadership, management, and support program, and was established to support schools in challenging communities by enhancing the capacity of school leaders to address the complex challenges in schools and to improve educational outcomes for students from challenging contexts at a state-wide level in Western Australia. The program focuses on building the capacity of school leadership teams to make informed evidence-

---

4. Retrieved with permissions from My School at https://www.myschool.edu.au/school/48470

based decisions, strategically plan and aim to improve student engagement and outcomes across the curriculum[5].

The first change implemented followed a whole school literacy audit which indicated a whole school approach was needed, as several different literacy programs were being used across the school. Building on the whole school literacy audit and extensive research for the most effective literacy program, Sounds-Write was selected.

One of the Fogarty partnerships was with Dyslexia-SPELD Foundation* (DSF), which offers literacy and clinical services to children and adults with specific learning disabilities to realize their greatest potential. The school engaged their services to assist with the implementation of the chosen whole school literacy program, Sounds-Write, and monitor the validity of the program, and to provide students with the best opportunity to leave primary school with more competent skills and knowledge to access the high school curriculum.

2. Implementation

On my arrival at the school in 2018, there were no identified programs to provide students with intervention. There were five different literacy programs being delivered at the school. Many of these were not evidence-based or consistent across the whole school.

Initially, I selected two highly competent education assistants for Sounds-Write training. After their training, I assisted them in developing an intervention program to support the learning needs of students at risk by delivering Sounds-Write one-to-one and in small groups up to four sessions a week. Funded and diagnosed students were the first priority and then those who were at academic risk of not being able to access the curriculum.

---

5. https://fogartyedvance.org.au/school-improvement-program

Chapter 7

In mid-2020, during the school holidays, all teachers completed the four-day Sounds-Write training course. In Western Australia we had been incredibly lucky at the time in not being affected by any COVID lockdowns and all our training was delivered face-to-face. A DSF trainer delivered the program at school and then was engaged to assist the school in ensuring that staff used the program with fidelity. Literacy coaches were appointed internally to support staff shoulder to shoulder in a coaching model. This approach was successful as staff were supported by colleagues in a non-threatening coaching context.

Meetings were conducted to explore the best programs and to ascertain staff 'buy-in'. In the 2020 July school holidays, leading into Semester 2, additional teachers were trained in the program. This also included key members of the school leadership team to enable them to have a greater understanding of the program. I had lessons, word lists photocopied and laminated, post notes, white boards, and markers, all ready for Day 1 of implementation.

Teachers from pre-primary* (children turning five by June 30) to Year 6 were required to complete placement tests and then commenced lessons based on student data. For example, in the Year 3 class, after assessment, students were placed at the beginning of the Extended Code*. After consultations with DSF trainers, and since the majority of students at NPS had significant gaps in Initial Code* knowledge, the introduction of the program proceeded at a reduced pace. To reduce the pressure for staff of a complete change in their literacy programs, teachers were asked to complete just one Sounds-Write activity (which in Sounds-Write are known as 'lessons') a day during the first week, two lessons (or activities) a day in the second week and three in the third week. This removed any anxiety about implementing Sounds-Write and by the end of the first week, teachers were asking if they could deliver more than one lesson.

In 2021, teachers again reassessed their students and placed them accordingly at their Sounds-Write level. Several new students were receiving one-to-one Sounds-Write intervention to close the gaps at this time, also. By 2022, I anticipate the Year 3 cohort would be able to commence at Extended Code. It is worth remembering that students at NPS have significant gaps in their learning due to their high levels of transiency and many come to NPS with patchy knowledge of the Initial Code.

Years 4 to 6 have now completed Extended Code and are working on polysyllabic and morphology lessons. However, staff continue to review phonics to address any gaps in their students' literacy understanding.

The IEC students are also taught the Sound-Write program. When students exit this program into the mainstream, accommodations need to be made as students are generally working at a lower level and pace due to them being at the early stages of acquiring standard Australian English.

In Kindergarten at NPS, teachers deliver the Heggerty Phonemic Awareness program. This program is a research-based curriculum of daily phonemic and phonological awareness lesson plans. In Semester 1 teachers at our school teach the PreLit program. PreLit is a systematic, skills-based early literacy program for Kindy* students who will be commencing in pre-primary* the following year. In Semester 2, 2021, Kindergarten* teachers start the foundation Sounds-Write lessons to enable students to have an understanding of the program and some of its processes before commencing pre-primary. Once in pre-primary, Sounds-Write Units 1 and 2 are retaught. Many of our students are from language backgrounds other than English so need the initial exposure before recapping the initial Sounds-Write lessons. This enables any students who are new in pre-primary to receive the initial lessons. Any students who need extension are given more activities in Unit 1 and 2 to keep them motivated and learning. We will be interested to see how students exposed to Sounds-Write in Semester 2 2021 engage in pre-primary in 2022.

Sounds-Write is a scripted, explicit instruction program that follows a scope and sequence*. This eliminates any teacher error that may otherwise creep into a program. Our school is an Explicit Direct Instruction (EDI) school. EDI is the delivery of strategically planned lessons that explicitly teach new concepts to mastery. As Sounds-Write has an explicit instruction delivery, it fits seamlessly into our school curriculum.

Chapter 7

3. Evaluation

Evidence indicates that the students who are receiving Sounds-Write interventions are 'closing the gap' where previously they were several years behind their peers in reading levels.

For this case study we use data from NAPLAN[*6] (National Assessment Program – Literacy and Numeracy) results for Year 3 and Year 5 for a small cohort of students from 2019 to 2021 (Table 1). Since the school has an extremely high transiency, approximately 51%, our stable cohort from Year 3 to Year 5 are seven students for spelling and writing, and eight for reading.

Table 1. Progress in spelling, reading, and writing from Year 3 to Year 5 (NAPLAN data)

Spelling - NAPLAN 2019 Year 3 to NAPLAN 2021 Year 5 (seven students)

	Year 3 2019	Year 5 2021	Progress	Value add	Effect size growth
Nollamara	397.67	523.29	126.0	40	2.40
Australian Mean	419.00	504.50	85.50		

Reading - NAPLAN 2019 Year 3 to NAPLAN 2021 Year 5 (eight students)

	Year 3 2019	Year 5 2021	Progress	Value add	Effect size growth
Nollamara	372.50	466.88	94.00	15	1.63
Australian Mean	432.00	511.60	79.60		

Writing - NAPLAN 2019 Year 3 to NAPLAN 2021 Year 5 (seven students)

	Year 3 2019	Year 5 2021	Progress	Value add	Effect size growth
Nollamara	372.50	469.29	62.00	5	2.49
Australian Mean	423.00	480.00	57.00		

---

6. "The National Assessment Program – Literacy and Numeracy (NAPLAN) is an annual national assessment for all students in Years 3, 5, 7, and 9. All students in these year levels are expected to participate in tests in reading, writing, language conventions (spelling, grammar and punctuation) and numeracy" https://www.nap.edu.au/naplan/faqs/naplan-- general.

Spelling shows an effect size growth of 2.4, and a staggering value add of 40. For reading, the effect size growth is also substantially above expectations at 1.63, with a value add of 15. For writing, the effect size growth is 2.49 and the value add is five. Considering that schools want to see an average growth of 0.8 and that a value add of five is considered good, these are impressive results.

We have noticed that our students are able to apply their word knowledge and write longer and more meaningful texts as they have confidence in their ability to spell and in turn write. Teachers are spending less time on spelling and moving into writing. Learning to write and reading to learn.

These data prove the benefit that Sounds-Write has had in the classroom as students at NPS are now proficiently able to spell, read, and write at a level that is comparable or better than the Australian mean.

4. Recommendations

Being able to implement Sounds-Write as a whole school literacy program is immensely beneficial. The gains in literacy were seen very quickly and across all year levels.

The first step to maintaining fidelity to the Sounds-Write program was a structural change of timetables, ensuring that every class was delivering Sounds-Write at 9 a.m. every morning. Students were encouraged to arrive at school on time and lateness continues to be addressed as a whole school.

A Sounds-Write trainer, engaged from outside the school, was timetabled to work with teachers, and their observations, which were timetabled twice a term, were followed by a meeting with staff. This enabled staff to discuss their progress and refine their skills and knowledge in Sounds-Write with an external coach. The school provided extra release time for teachers so that this meeting did not occur in their 'duties other than teaching' time as well as 'buying in' the services of the DSF coach.

Chapter 7

This semester, several Sounds-Write teacher experts have been identified and timetabled so teachers are able to engage with their peers, providing a non-threatening supportive coaching approach.

The introduction of new pedagogy is just the first step. To ensure staff are constantly upskilling themselves, they are attending a refresher course six months after their initial training.

Introducing new pedagogy has not been without its challenges, however, staff have been able to see in a very short time frame the improvement in students' literacy. This has resulted in a reduced teacher workload, as well as ensuring all students from Kindergarten to Year 6, including those in the IEC, are exposed to a consistent teaching approach.

8 Princecroft Primary School, Warminster, England

Anita Harley[1]

1. Context

Princecroft Primary School is a state primary school located in the rural, historic market town of Warminster in the county of Wiltshire, England. The school is one form entry and teaches children aged four to eleven across seven classes. We currently have 175 children on roll with 40% Free School Meals[*2] (FSM), 14% Special Educational Needs (SEN), 5% English as an Additional Language (EAL). Languages spoken are Polish, Chinese Mandarin, Bulgarian, Somali, and Bengali. The local deprivation factor* is -0.214.

2. Implementation

Prior to the implementation of Sounds-Write at the end of 2016, children in Year 1 were not consistently achieving national standards in reading shown by the Phonics Screening Check* (PSC) scores. Due to such low levels of decoding and continually achieving below national averages, we decided as a school that we needed a consistent approach that could help support our children better with their phonics.

Sounds-Write was first introduced into Princecroft in June 2016. To begin with, only the Reception and Year 1 teachers were trained. Over the following year, all staff at the school received training. This included all teachers, teaching

---

1. Princecroft Primary School, Warminster, England; aharley@princecroft.wilts.sch.uk

2. An explanation for terms followed by an asterisk can be found in the glossary: https://doi.org/10.14705/rpnet.2022.55.1367

How to cite: Harley, A. (2022). Princecroft Primary School, Warminster, England. In A. Beaven, A. Comas-Quinn & N. Hinton (Eds), *Systematic synthetic phonics: case studies from Sounds-Write practitioners* (pp. 79-86). Research-publishing.net. https://doi.org/10.14705/rpnet.2022.55.1362

assistants, and office staff. Since its implementation, new staff have been trained to ensure that consistency and maximum impact can be had from those that support children in their reading. All staff have been trained face-to-face and some staff completed the Sounds-Write Revisited course online during lockdown in 2021.

Sounds-Write is taught daily throughout the school. The Initial Code* is taught in Reception. In Year 1 and Year 2, the Extended Code* is taught. Throughout Lower Key Stage* 2 (LKS2), the Extended Code is built upon through learning more complex polysyllabic words alongside National Curriculum* expectations for spelling. In Upper Key Stage 2 (UKS2), phonics teaching is enhanced through the teaching of etymology and morphology, with children analysing the spellings of words. All Sounds-Write lessons are taught to the whole class so that every child has the opportunity to develop their reading and spelling. Interventions are then taught in addition to this with children receiving the Sounds-Write approach in smaller groups to ensure accelerated progress. Where necessary, one-to-one teaching is used to support individual needs.

As a school, we have endeavoured to ensure that the Sounds-Write approach is taught with fidelity. Teachers are held accountable for using scripts in every lesson to ensure that consistency is kept across the school. Having all staff trained allowed us to use a range of staff members to support children with reading, as errors would be corrected in line with the Sounds-Write approach. In the early months of school, parents and carers are invited to Sounds-Write lessons to watch how their children are taught, along with teacher support of how to help their children read at home.

Table 1 shows our PSC scores from 2014 to 2019. After three years of teaching using Sounds-Write, we have started to see progress in our PSC scores and, as a school, we are achieving percentages that are in line with national standards. There was a decrease in the percentage passing the PSC from 2018-2019. This was largely due to a high number of children joining the class from other schools late in their Reception year or during Year 1. They joined Princecroft School working below the national standard in reading and writing.

Table 1. Phonics Screening Check scores

Year	Princecroft	National
2014	64%	74%
2015	70%	77%
2016	60%	77%
Implementation of Sounds-Write		
2017	79%	81%
2018	94%	82%
2019	80%	82%

This case study will focus around the children who were in Year 2 during the academic year 2020-2021. These children were aged six to seven when the data was collected. It is important to note that these children have experienced disruption, including lockdowns, due to the Covid-19 pandemic, resulting in large amounts of time working from home.

Since starting in Reception, they have been taught using Sounds-Write so, by the end of Year 2, they had been taught the programme for three years. These Sounds-Write lessons were delivered to the whole class for 30 minutes a day. For those who were in need of additional intervention, they received this three times a week for 15 minutes in small groups with a teaching assistant who was trained in delivering Sounds-Write. These interventions were a way of filling any learning gaps the children had and used the Sounds-Write approach and the Sounds-Write scripted lessons to teach the sounds they did not know.

To ensure consistency throughout the lockdowns, children were given Sounds-Write activities to complete at home. This included syllabifying polysyllabic words and sorting words based on the spelling of a target sound. There was an expectation that children would say the sounds as they read and wrote the words. In the most recent lockdown, teachers used daily live lessons to teach Sounds-Write to ensure learning was maximised. Teachers continued to use the scripts to deliver their lessons and taught from units already covered to ensure that children were secure in the sounds they had learnt. The level of engagement for these Sounds-Write lessons was high on a daily basis.

Chapter 8

3. Evaluation

Due to the pandemic, the children in this class did not take the PSC in Year 1 (June 2020). Instead they took the PSC in October 2021 (see Table 2). The mean score was 34.9 with 10% achieving the full 40 marks. The pass mark for the PSC is 32 out of 40. Child 19 did not take the PSC due to significant SEN.

Table 2. Phonics Screening Check scores – October 2021

Child	Score
C1	39
C2	37
C3	32
C4	34
C5	35
C6	33
C7	32
C8	38
C9	35
C10	32
C11	33
C12	39
C13	33
C14	38
C15	22
C16	33
C17	40
C18	40
C19	n/a
C20	38
C21	34

Of the 21 children in the cohort, ten were eligible for Pupil Premium*, two received SEN support in school, one had an Education Health Care Plan*, and two spoke EAL. Table 3 shows a breakdown of the PSC scores for these groups of children, showing the percentage of children passing (achieving a score of 32/40 or more) in each of the groups. Our school data for October 2021 is presented alongside the national data for 2019.

Table 3. Phonics Screening Check breakdown – % passing

	National (2019)	Princecroft (2021)
All students	82%	90% (19/21)
Students eligible for Pupil Premium*	71%	90% (9/10)
Students not eligible for Pupil Premium	84%	91% (10/11)
SEN Support		100% (2/2)
EHCP		0% (0/1)
EAL		100% (2/2)

In addition to the PSC, this cohort also took Young's *Parallel Spelling Tests** (PST) and the KS1 Reading SATs* paper in June 2021. Table 4 shows the data from both of these tests for this cohort.

Young's *Parallel Spelling Tests* scores show that the children's ability to spell is high. Of the 23 children tested, 20 children achieved a higher spelling age than their actual age. Of the other three, one was absent during the test, one had a spelling age equal to their chronological age, and the other child had a spelling age of only one month behind their chronological age.

In summer 2021, it was not an expectation for Year 2 to take the SATs papers. However, to assess the children's progress, we decided that it was a good indicator of how children's learning had progressed throughout KS1. Without the ability to decode, children cannot access this assessment. Through the precise lessons provided by the Sounds-Write programme and dedication to the consistent delivery of the Sounds-Write programme throughout lockdowns from the school, we have been able to achieve these reading SATs scores. Eight children were able to achieve a Greater Depth standard which means that they are working above the expected standard for their age. The SATs results provide clear evidence that the children's decoding skills through using Sounds-Write are strong and well-embedded. In both of these assessments many of the children achieved at or above the expected standard.

Chapter 8

Table 4. Young's *Parallel Spelling Tests* and Reading SATs Scores Year 2 - June 2021

	Actual Age year & months	Young's PST		Reading SATs			Notes
		Spelling Age year & months	Raw Score (max 32)	Paper 1 (max 20)	Paper 2 (max 20)	Total (max 40)	
C1	7.8	8.1	19	11	10	21	
C2	7.9	10.5	32	20	19	39	
C3	6.10	11.0	33	16	16	32	
C4	7.5	8.0	18	13	11	24	
C5	7.1	7.1	12	8	6	14	Pupil Premium, EAL, SEN
C6	7.0	7.7	16	10	6	16	Military Family[3]
C7	6.11	7.4	14	19	5	24	
C8	7.9	9.0	25	19	19	38	
C9	7.1	7.7	16	7	9	16	Pupil Premium
C10	7.4	10.5	32	19	20	39	Pupil Premium
C11	7.0	9.3	27	19	18	37	
C12	6.11	8.8	24	14	8	24	Military Family
C13	6.11	7.7	16	13	11	24	Military Family
C14	6.11	8.8	24	14	16	30	
C15	6.10	8.6	23	19	14	33	
C16	7.3	9.3	27	18	17	35	
C17	7.1	9.1	26	18	18	36	
C18	7.7	9.9	30	20	17	37	Pupil Premium
C19	7.5	Absent	Absent	18	8	26	SEN
C20	7.7	9.9	30	19	17	36	
C21	7.0	8.2	20	19	17	36	
C22	7.4	8.0	18	8	9	17	
C23	7.6	7.5	15	13	2	15	Pupil Premium

3. Princecroft is close to a military base. Children from military families often do not settle into school as well as other children as they move frequently. This can affect progress and learning behaviours.

4. Recommendations

Sounds-Write has improved the teaching of decoding with associated improvements in reading and significantly improved spelling. It has given us a consistent approach that all teachers and adults working with children can use and allows the children to move through the school, building on their knowledge without having to learn a new approach.

After teaching the programme for an extended period of time, we have learnt how important it is to stick to the original wording of the scripts. Going back to these regularly and checking against them as you teach is necessary as it is easy to drift away, adding in additional language that is not important and can inadvertently confuse the students. Having consistent, high expectations in Sounds-Write lessons and being precise in language is essential. This goes as far as the expectations of presentation on boards. For example, children must draw lines as instructed to provide the most effective scaffold to support learning and support the teacher in identifying mistakes.

Sounds-Write provides a clear teaching structure to teach the phonetic code for reading and spelling. It is important that enough time is given for children to really embed new learning. We teach a new sound and the ways in which it can be spelled over an extended period of time so that once children can recognise it, they can revisit it through reading and retrieval practice. This has given our students more chances to cover the new sound-spelling correspondences they have been taught and embed them to provide fluency. This interleaving process also supports them in using more challenging skills with previously learnt units. Having high expectations of what children can achieve is crucial but not progressing through the programme until they have successfully achieved the skills and knowledge required will provide the best learning environment for the children.

As with any phonics programme, it is essential that all staff are committed to teaching it and have the required subject knowledge. The training for the Sounds-Write programme provides in-depth subject knowledge for teachers, which supports them in their phonics lessons. However, knowledge can be easily forgotten if not revisited. Therefore, it is important that school leaders provide regular support to teachers to ensure confidence in the teaching of Sounds-Write. Support in subject knowledge is important for KS2 colleagues as Sounds-Write provides lessons that can be used throughout the primary age range. To ensure children become competent readers and spellers they need to continue to be taught phonics throughout KS2. Sounds-Write provides additional training in phonics that is specific to Years 3-6, which most of our KS2 teachers have now undertaken. This course shows teachers how to progress their Sounds-Write teaching when they have built up the essential skills through teaching the lessons provided from the original Sounds-Write training.

In our experience, we found that ensuring parents are as well-informed as possible about the approaches of Sounds-Write can then maximise the learning at home. Sounds-Write provides a very helpful online Course for Parents (and Carers), which the school encourages them to complete.

Our aims for the future are to develop the teaching of Sounds-Write in our new Nursery (age three). This will be an important step to find out what is most beneficial for our youngest learners to experience before they start Reception. We also need to continue to develop the planning and coverage in KS2 to ensure there is enough challenge and review of previous learning. The progression throughout Early Years Foundation Stage and KS1 is clear and we now need to have this in place for KS2.

9 Selby Community Primary School, North Yorkshire, England

Emma Darwin[1]

1. Context

Selby Community Primary School is an average-sized primary school with a two-form entry*[2] situated a short distance from the centre of Selby in North Yorkshire. Selby is amongst the ten percent most deprived areas in England. It is located within the Selby North Ward, with 30% of children living in poverty, which is higher than the national average. Selby District has the second highest health inequality in North Yorkshire[3].

At present, Selby Community Primary has 335 children on roll from Nursery to Year 6 (ages two to eleven). The school has a large majority of students from a White British background and 23% have English as an Additional Language* (EAL), mainly from Eastern European countries. Across the whole school, 36% are currently accessing free school meals*, which is well above the national average. Although the proportion of students who have special educational needs and/or disabilities is average overall, the proportion that have an Education and Health Care Plan* (EHCP) is above average. The number of students who join or leave the school part-way through their primary education is high. The school has Healthy Schools status[4], the Basic Skills Quality Mark[5],

---

1. Selby Community Primary School, Selby, England; darwine@selby.ac.uk

2. An explanation for terms followed by an asterisk can be found in the glossary: https://doi.org/10.14705/rpnet.2022.55.1367

3. North Yorkshire County Council 2019 Strategic Needs Assessment: https://hub.datanorthyorkshire.org/dataset/ef082317-37ed-428f-b849-740c4587fe06/resource/9b8b6efe-7808-4b37-a29d-7312f498395c/download/selby-2019.pdf

4. https://www.gov.uk/government/publications/healthy-schools-rating-scheme

5. https://www.tribalgroup.com/education-services/quality-mark

How to cite: Darwin, E. (2022). Selby Community Primary School, North Yorkshire, England. In A. Beaven, A. Comas-Quinn & N. Hinton (Eds), *Systematic synthetic phonics: case studies from Sounds-Write practitioners* (pp. 87-95). Research-publishing.net. https://doi.org/10.14705/rpnet.2022.55.1363

Chapter 9

the Dyslexia Quality Mark[6], and has received the UNICEF Rights Respecting School[7] award along with being a Talk 4 Writing[8] training school. In 2016, Selby Community Primary became a designated National Support School[9] in recognition of our strong record in successfully providing school-to-school support to others that have needed our help.

2. Implementation

The school embarked on their Sounds-Write journey in the summer of 2016, when senior leaders and the Early Years Foundation team trained to implement the programme in the new academic year that September. Prior to the implementation of Sounds-Write, the school had consistently reached and often exceeded the national average for the Phonics Screening Check since its implementation in 2007. However, senior leaders had noted that the weakest readers remained weak by the end of Key Stage 2*, and often made little meaningful progress in phonics or spelling. They had seen the impact of Sounds-Write as a whole school initiative when they visited Saint George's Church of England Primary School (Battersea, London) and wanted to implement the same whole school teaching in Selby, starting with the new cohort beginning in Reception. The school were lucky to have face-to-face training with one of the founders of the Sounds-Write programme, and all of the team were eager to get started once trained.

From the initial implementation in 2016, the school has now trained seventeen teaching staff via various face-to-face courses and seven teaching staff via the online route. Over the past five years, Sounds-Write has been implemented and delivered across the whole school from Nursery through to Year 6. As part of

---

6. https://www.bdadyslexia.org.uk/advice/educators/creating-a-dyslexia-friendly-school/dyslexia-friendly-school-awards

7. https://www.unicef.org.uk/rights-respecting-schools/

8. https://www.talk4writing.com

9. National Support Schools (NSS) are designated by the UK's Department for Education to support schools in challenging circumstances through the use of their skills, expertise and experience.

the Quality First Teaching[10] at Tier* 1, the school delivers whole class Sounds-Write sessions for 30 minutes each day from Reception to Year 2. Within these year groups, if a child needs further support at Tier 2, interventions take place in supported small groups, whilst Tier 3 interventions are delivered one-to-one and contain increased targeted support. From Year 3 onwards, Sounds-Write sessions are delivered three times a week focusing on spelling, morphology, and etymology. Intervention groups continue to be provided where needed at Tier 2 and 3 throughout Key Stage 2.

3. Evaluation

This data set was first taken in the summer of 2018, when our current Year 4 students were in Year 1. These children were the first in the school to have been taught phonics via the Sounds-Write programme consistently from their Reception year (2016-2017). The sessions had been delivered daily as a whole class with additional small intervention groups for those requiring extra practice at Tier 2 and 3 throughout the week. On a recommendation from Sounds-Write, the school decided to use Young's *Parallel Spelling Tests** to monitor the spelling progression throughout the school.

The first data set below (Table 1) shows the children's chronological age compared to their spelling age generated from their raw scores in Young's *Parallel Spelling Tests*. The last column identifies the children who were accessing Tier 2 and 3 intervention and those children who had EAL, as well as those who were new to the school, and so had not received Sounds-Write in their Reception year.

The data set shows that 100% of the children matched or exceeded their chronological age for spelling by the end of Year 1, with 76% of the class achieving a spelling age twelve months greater than their chronological age. Furthermore, 38% of the children achieved a score 36 months greater than their

---

10. https://cyps.northyorks.gov.uk/sites/default/files/SEND/IES%20landing%20page/Quality%20First%20Teaching%20Guidance.pdf

chronological age, and five children out of 42 achieved a score of 42 months or more above their age.

Breaking this data set down further, we looked closely at the attainment of the EAL children. Amazingly, 100% of the EAL cohort, with the exception of Child U, achieved a spelling score nine months greater than their current age and 55% of the group achieved a score of eighteen months greater than their current age. Child U joined the school in the summer term, having moved from a country outside of Europe. The country in which he had lived did not start formal schooling until the age of seven, so his first experience of a school was with us. At that point he had not been taught Sounds-Write previously so did not have the code knowledge, conceptual knowledge, or skills required to attempt the spelling test.

Table 1. Year 1 Young's *Parallel Spelling Tests* results July 2018

Child	Chronological Age (Years and months)	Spelling Age (Years)	Difference in months	Additional information
A	6.2	7.7	+17	
B	6.6	7.4	+10	SEND - SpLD[11]/Tier 3
C	6.10	7	+3	EAL SEND - SpLD/Tier 3
D	6.7	7.3	+8	
E	5.10	8.1	+26	EAL New to school
F	6.0	11.1	+61	EAL
G	6.6	9.8	+38	EAL
H	6.2	7.5	+15	
I	6.4	7.7	+15	EAL
J	6.9	7.8	+11	
K	6.2	6.9	+7	SEND - SpLD/Tier 3

---

11. Special Educational Needs and Disabilities & Specific Learning Difficulties: https://www.dyslexia.uk.net/specific-learning-difficulties/

L	6.1	8.2	+25	
M	6.5	7.8	+15	
N	6.4	9.3	+35	
O	6.6	9.0	+30	EAL New to school
P	6.7	9.3	+32	
Q	6.4	7.8	+16	
R	6.4	10.2	+46	EAL
S	6.4	8.6	+26	
T	6.0	8.4	+28	EAL
U	-	-		EAL SEND - SpLD/ Tier 3 New to school
V	6.8	10.6	+43	EAL
W	6.7	8.4	+21	
X	6.3	10	+45	
Y	6.2	7.3	+13	
Z	6.8	8.5	+21	
AA	6.2	7.8	+18	EAL
BB	6.0	8	+24	
CC	6.1	8	+23	
DD	5.10	7.3	+17	EAL
EE	6.9	6.9	0	SEND - SpLD/ Tier 3
FF	6.1	8.8	+31	EAL
GG	6.3	6.9	+3	SEND - SpLD/ Tier 3
HH	6.8	7.8	+12	EAL
II	6.9	8.6	+21	EAL
JJ	6.0	6.5	+5	
KK	6.7	8.2	+19	
LL	6.4	10.2	+46	
MM	6.6	8.5	+23	EAL
NN	6.6	9.8	+38	EAL
OO	6.7	7	+5	SEND - SpLD/ Tier 3
PP	6.3	6.9	+6	
QQ	6.0	7.4	+16	

Chapter 9

This cohort transitioned into Year 2 and continued to receive daily Sounds-Write whole class sessions, with additional interventions continuing for those children who needed extra support. They completed their Standardised Assessment Tests (SATs) towards the end of this year and the school's judgements were moderated by the Local Education Authority[12]. Incredibly, 47% of this cohort reached the higher standard for reading and writing.

In Year 3, the children received three whole class Sounds-Write sessions focusing on spelling. Unfortunately, halfway through the year, like for many others across the world, their education was suddenly disrupted due to the Covid-19 global pandemic. The children were only into their second term when school closed and teaching moved to online homeschooling. Due to the high level of deprivation in our area, online learning was very difficult for many of our families as they did not have the technology and skills to support online learning at home. Laptops were donated to every family within the school but the impact of the pandemic was manifesting itself in many different ways for our families.

Along with other subjects within the Year 3 curriculum, regular Sounds-Write sessions were provided through the online platform for the children to access. These took the form of slide presentations and spelling tests. Unfortunately, the pandemic forced another school closure for this group of children part-way through their Year 4 schooling, with online learning re-commencing over the winter months.

The data set below in Table 2 shows the chronological ages and the spelling ages of the same children at the end of Year 4, taken in July 2021 after a full term of being back in school. By this point, Children F, M, and BB had left the school, moving into another area. Although the children had experienced two very disruptive years, Young's *Parallel Spelling Tests* results showed that 78% of the children matched or exceeded their chronological age for spelling by the end of Year 4, with 60% of the class achieving a spelling age twelve months greater than their current age. Looking closer at the attainment of the same EAL children

---

12. Local education authorities (LEAs) in England and Wales were responsible for education within their jurisdictions, but have been progressively phased out and their responsibilities moved to local authorities.

we tracked in Year 1, amazingly 94% of this group of children achieved their chronological age or more, with 81% achieving a score twelve months greater than their chronological age. Unfortunately, the children who had been receiving additional quality intervention in school due to their additional needs were not able to access this during the online learning. The pandemic was manifesting many different issues within our families, not just the barrier of not being able to access a computer. The level of support that these children needed could not be provided during these difficult times and unfortunately this impacted on the progress made by B, D, U, Y, EE, GG, JJ, OO, and PP. Since September 2021, we have had a higher level teaching assistant take these children, and others, for small group Sounds-Write interventions every afternoon. At time of writing, staff and student absences due to Covid are still high and unpredictable, so it is not always possible for these groups to go ahead.

Table 2. Year 4 Young's *Parallel Spelling Tests* July 2021

Child	Chronological Age (Years)	Spelling Age (Years)	Difference (months)	Additional information
A	9.2	9.6	+4	
B	9.6	7.7	-25	SEND - SpLD - Tier 3/2
C	9.10	10.5	+7	EAL
D	9.7	9.4	-3	Tier 2 Intervention 2020/2021
E	8.10	10.7	+21	EAL
F	-	-	-	-
G	9.6	12	+30	EAL
H	9.2	9.6	+4	
I	9.4	11.4	+24	EAL
J	9.9	11	+15	
K	9.2	10	+10	
L	9.1	11.4	+27	
M	-	-	-	
N	9.4	11.7	+27	
O	9.6	12.7	+37	EAL
P	9.7	12.3	+32	
Q	9.4	11.7	+27	
R	9.4	12.3	+35	EAL

S	9.4	12.3	+35	
T	9	11	+24	EAL
U	9.3	7	-27	SEND - SpLD - Tier 3/2 EAL
V	9.8	10.6	+10	EAL
W	9.7	11.2	+19	
X	9.3	13.2	+47	
Y	9.2	7.5	-21	SEND - SpLD - Tier 3/2
Z	9.8	10.7	+11	
AA	9.2	11.7	+29	EAL
BB	-	-	-	-
CC	9.1	11.4	+27	
DD	8.10	13.7	+57	EAL
EE	9.9	7.5	-28	SEND - SpLD - Tier 3/2
FF	9.1	13.2	+49	EAL
GG	9.3	7.5	-22	SEND - SpLD - Tier 3/2
HH	9.8	11	+17	EAL
II	9.9	13.7	+46	EAL
JJ	9.5	7.5	-24	SEND - SpLD - Tier 3/2
KK	9.7	12	+29	
LL	9.4	12.3	+35	
MM	9.6	13.2	+44	EAL
NN	9.6	13.7	+49	EAL
OO	9.6	7	-30	SEND - SpLD - Tier 3/2
PP	9.3	8.6	-9	Tier 2 Intervention 2020/2021
QQ	9.0	9.2	+2	

4. Recommendations

The consistency of the delivery of the Sounds-Write scripts has been key to the success for our children. Ensuring that all teaching staff within a year group were trained helped them to peer support and refine their practice in its implementation. Peer monitoring has helped the staff gain confidence to teach the Sounds-Write scripts with fidelity. Teaching the same content to the whole class ensures no child is left behind with their learning, and intervention groups should be put in place for those that need extra practice. Sounds-Write advocates teaching the whole class together, using booster sessions where needed, and this is what we did, rather than grouping and teaching different content to different ability groups. We now have an advanced teaching assistant who delivers these booster sessions to ensure consistency of support throughout the school.

Because of the high proportion of EAL children in the class, we used visual images as part of our Sounds-Write teaching in Reception in order to support their understanding of the words that they were being asked to build/read. In addition to the main class teaching, some of the EAL children had vocabulary development sessions to pre-teach vocabulary needed for the sessions. Being a Talk 4 Writing school has helped enormously with vocabulary building for our EAL learners, and both these programmes work seamlessly together.

10. Speech-language therapist, Munich, Germany: one-to-one intervention

Shelley Hornberger[1]

1. Context

As an Australian trained speech-language pathologist, I have worked in public settings in both New Zealand and the United Kingdom before starting an independent speech-language therapy practice in Munich, Germany in 2019. In my current role, I support English-speaking students aged three to eighteen with speech, language, and literacy disorders, most of whom attend private English-medium international schools in Munich.

The majority of my caseload are simultaneous bilinguals, with English being their primary language in education. Many students have had a varied educational background, often having attended public and/or international schools in other countries before arriving in Munich, meaning they each present a unique history of prior language and literacy programmes and support.

2. Implementation

I trained in Sounds-Write in mid-2020 through the online training course and use the programme in a one-to-one intervention context, mainly with students in the upper primary age group who have been referred due to concerns regarding their language and literacy progress.

---

1. Speech & Language Services, Munich, Germany; shelley@speechlanguageservices.de

How to cite: Hornberger, S. (2022). Speech-language therapist, Munich, Germany: one-to-one intervention. In A. Beaven, A. Comas-Quinn & N. Hinton (Eds), *Systematic synthetic phonics: case studies from Sounds-Write practitioners* (pp. 97-104). Research-publishing.net. https://doi.org/10.14705/rpnet.2022.55.1364

© 2022 Shelley Hornberger (CC BY)

Chapter 10

Due to the COVID pandemic and related school closures, to date I have been predominantly delivering Sounds-Write online via teletherapy using Smart Notebook software and the Zoom videoconferencing platform.

Students attend weekly individual therapy sessions for 45 minutes or one hour, and parents are requested to attend the online teletherapy sessions with their child. Individualised home practice packs are provided after each session for parents to complete during the week with their child. Parents are advised prior to commencing Sounds-Write that regular home practice is essential for maximising progress and that their child will be provided with a weekly home practice programme.

The home practice programme provided for Case A in this case study consisted of three to four daily practice plans per week, with each day's practice consisting of four different activities. As Case A's parent attended every therapy session, both for online and face-to-face sessions, she became very familiar with the Sounds-Write teaching approach and was able to support him effectively at home through the home programme. The activities included reading decodable texts/books for fluency practice, Sounds-Write lessons 3, 4, 6, 7, 8, 9, and 10, worksheets from the Phonics Books UK and Sounds-Write workbooks, spelling quizzes, and dictations. Case A's parent was requested to scan and email the completed home practice to the speech-language therapist two days before his next session to monitor progress. The amount and frequency of practice Case A was able to complete at home varied depending on the work, home schooling, and other commitments of the family, however, on average Case A completed three practice sessions at home per week through each school term.

Case A was referred for speech-language therapy support aged eight years and five months, due to his significant and ongoing literacy difficulties. Case A has a family history of speech, language, and literacy difficulties and was reported to have found learning to read and write difficult since starting school. His family arranged for a private reading assessment in Year 2 which did not provide a formal diagnosis of dyslexia but did conclude he showed a pattern of difficulties consistent with dyslexia. At the point of referral, Case A had received the following previous phonics instruction.

- The Letters & Sounds programme for three years (Reception to Year 2) in his mainstream school in the UK.

- Approximately eighteen months of private tutoring in the UK using Oxford Reading Tree stories and workbooks.

- The Reading Horizons programme (a print-to-sound derivative of Orton-Gillingham, which includes a complex strategy of marking spelling patterns in a word with symbols in order to decode) with the school Special Educational Needs Coordinator at his international school in Munich for one year (Year 3 to Year 4).

Case A was assessed using the Test of Integrated Language and Literacy Skills[*2] alongside other clinical assessments of his language and literacy skills at the time of referral in September 2019, and again, aged ten years and two months in June 2021.

Case A was seen individually on a weekly-fortnightly basis over this nearly two-year time period through a mixture of face-to-face and online sessions, excluding a three-month break during the therapist's maternity leave. Case A completed three to four individualised home practice sessions each week.

At the time of initial assessment, Case A presented with significant difficulties in the following areas.

- Significant phonemic awareness difficulties, including difficulty identifying rhyming words consistently, segmenting words into syllables, as well as blending, segmenting or manipulating sounds in words.

---

2. https://tillstest.com/about/; an explanation for terms followed by an asterisk can be found in the glossary: https://doi.org/10.14705/rpnet.2022.55.1367

- Many gaps in his code and conceptual knowledge. He relied predominantly on a visual memorisation strategy to learn words and did not show a solid conceptual understanding that words are made up of sounds and that letters are used to represent these sounds.

- Difficulty knowing how to approach reading a word that was new to him. When presented with a word he had not already visually memorised, he would either use the first letter and visual length of the word to guess the word, would spell the word out loud using its letter names, or quote the spelling rule/pattern he thought would apply.

- Difficulty accurately representing the sounds within words when spelling, due to his phonemic awareness difficulties and reduced alphabetic code knowledge. He relied on using inefficient visual memorisation strategies to remember word spellings which often resulted in incorrectly sequenced or missing letters, or letter combinations that are not allowable in English.

- Difficulty comprehending written texts, primarily due to his significant decoding difficulties.

Case A's oral language skills remained largely within the borderline average range; however, his vocabulary knowledge was below that of his same-aged peers.

Case A's sessions over the first two school terms targeted his significant phonemic awareness difficulties (segmenting, blending, phoneme deletion, and manipulation skills) and consolidated Phases 2 to 4 of the Letters and Sounds programme. Following the speech-language therapist's training in Sounds-Write in mid-2020, Case A then received the Sounds-Write programme exclusively for the duration of the 2020/21 school year starting with the Bridging Units at the end of the Initial Code*, followed by the Extended Code* and Polysyllabic Words.

He did not receive further reading support from school over this period whilst distance learning was in place during the pandemic.

3. Evaluation

Table 1 below includes brief descriptions of the TILLS subtests* and shows Case A's standard scores by language level (Sound/Word and Sentence/Discourse). Subtest standard scores between seven and thirteen are ±1 standard deviation of the mean score and are considered within the 'average' range. Subtest scores of thirteen or above are considered 'above average', subtest scores of six or below are considered 'below average'. Subtest scores of seven are considered 'borderline average' and are categorised as weaknesses.

At the time of initial assessment aged eight years and five months (September 2019), Case A presented with skills below the average range for all written language subtests and many subtests were unable to be administered as his decoding/spelling skills were not sufficient to complete the test. At the time of review assessment aged ten years and two months (June 2021), Case A presented with skills within the average range for four out of the seven written language subtests (Nonword Reading, Reading Fluency, Written Expression-Discourse, and Written Expression-Sentence), one was in the borderline average range (Nonword Spelling) and two were below the average range (Written Expression-Word score and Reading Comprehension) (see Table 1 below).

Case A made significant progress over the course of the intervention period in his code knowledge, phonemic skills (blending, segmenting, and manipulating) and his conceptual understanding of the reversible nature of the code. His reading accuracy is now age-appropriate; however, his decoding does remain effortful and continues to impact his capacity to draw meaning from the texts he is reading, resulting in his below-average reading comprehension score. His spelling attempts are now consistently phonetically plausible and there is no longer evidence of sound sequence errors or illegal letter combinations. These qualitative improvements were however not accounted for in the scoring of the Written Expression-Word subtest, as responses are scored as either correct or incorrect spelling, so his overall score of zero does not fully capture the changes in his spelling ability. He continues to require frequent, spaced retrieval practice to firmly establish the correct spellings of words in his long-term memory.

Chapter 10

Table 1. Case A's TILLS scores in September 2019 and June 2021

	Written Language Subtests	Standard Score Sept 2019	Standard Score June 2021
Sound/Word Level Skills	**Nonword Reading (NW Read)** Assesses reading decoding ability, which contributes to reading comprehension and academic success.	3	8
	Reading Fluency (RF) Assesses ability to read real words in context automatically, providing an index of reading proficiency in context.	0	8
	Nonword Spelling (NW Spell) Assesses ability to spell novel words using knowledge of sounds, morphemes, and letter patterns.	6	7
	Written Expression-Word score (WE-Word) Assesses ability to select and spell real words in meaningful contexts, which is essential for producing written language.	Not assessed due to significant difficulties with decoding and spelling	0
Sentence/Discourse Level Skills	**Reading Comprehension (RC)** Assesses the ability to read and understand written language with complex academic syntax and relational terminology and to monitor language comprehension, as required for learning from texts	Did not meet basal criteria to administer due to significant decoding difficulties	6
	Written Expression-Discourse (WE-Disc) Assesses ability to include complete information when rewriting a story, reflecting complex integrated skills for understanding and producing written language.	Not assessed due to significant difficulties with decoding and spelling	11
	Written Expression-Sentence (WE-Sent) Assesses ability to combine short sentences into more complex ones when rewriting a story, reflecting complex integrated skills for understanding and formulating written language.	Not assessed due to significant difficulties with decoding and spelling	8

Case A now describes reading and spelling as being "simple but not easy", explaining that he now finds the reversible nature of the code simple to understand but remembering the correct spellings of sounds continues to be "not easy".

Case A's parents provided the following feedback:

> "[Case A] has made amazing progress using the Sounds-Write programme with Shelley over the last 2 years! We are so impressed with his progress and thankful that we started the program when we did. The strategies used in Sounds-Write and the way the program is written, it is like it's been tailor-made to [Case A]'s needs. We are so happy to have found Shelley and a program that works for [Case A] as all previous methods we tried didn't help at all. [Case A] would often feel frustrated and not make any progress, which was really difficult as a parent to watch. [Case A] is now like a different child, he is so much more confident in his abilities and has made amazing progress. It is so lovely to see and we owe it all to Shelley and the Sounds-Write programme. I will be recommending Sounds-Write to his new school when we return to the UK. A very happy parent!".

4. Recommendations

The response to the Sounds-Write programme has been overwhelmingly positive from Case A's parents, his class teacher, and the school's Special Educational Needs Coordinator. The results of this case study also show that significant progress can be achieved with the Sounds-Write programme being delivered through online learning, using software such as Smart Notebook.

For clinicians using Sounds-Write in a one-to-one intervention context, the following points should be considered:

- Engaged and supportive parents and school staff are vital, however obtaining initial 'buy-in' from parents and school staff may be difficult if they are reluctant for the student to commence yet another phonics programme or if they are unfamiliar with the Sounds-Write programme itself. Having a clear understanding of the main points of difference between Sounds-Write and other literacy programmes and being able to confidently explain these to parents and school staff, as well as keeping pre- and post-intervention data to demonstrate the progress the student has made following the Sounds-Write approach is key.

- Identifying ways to maintain high levels of student engagement over the course of an intervention period and frequent practice between one-to-one sessions is also crucial. For Case A in this study, the following contributed to his level of engagement across the intervention period: having a supportive and involved parent, ensuring he was not withdrawn from his favourite school subjects for his one-to-one sessions, identifying a long-term goal that motivated him (e.g. being able to read a chapter book), making his progress clearly visible to him using tables and charts, allowing him a choice in reading materials based on his interests, encouraging him to take ownership of his own home practice schedule, and fostering a growth mindset.

- Regular meetings should take place between parents, school, and the clinician to facilitate communication about targets, progress, and implementation of the programme.

- Students should be provided with clear, easy-to-follow home practice plans which are achievable for parents to support and provide the student with the essential frequency of practice they require.

11 St George's Church of England Primary School, London, England

Alexandra Hammond[1]

1. Context

I work as a teacher for St George's Church of England Primary School, a one-form state primary school in Battersea, London, where I have taught in Key Stage[*2] 1 (KS1) and used Sounds-Write since 2017. I am the KS1 leader and the phonics lead at the school.

With a total of 222 students in 2020/2021, St George's Primary School had 51.8% of students whose first language is not English (versus an average of 20.9% across English mainstream primary schools), 47.7% of students eligible for free school meals* (versus 23.5% across English mainstream primary schools), and 20.7% of children on the Special Educational Needs and Disabilities (SEND) register – 10.8% of whom had an Education, Health and Care Plan* (EHCP) (versus 12.6% of students with SEND support across mainstream primary schools and 2% with EHCPs)[3]. St George's Primary School was rated as Good by OFSTED* (2019) and the report deemed that

> "adults ensure that pupils secure their phonics knowledge early on. For example, the highly effective teaching of phonics is enabling pupils in Year 1 to identify the six spelling choices for the sound 'o'.

---

1. St George's Church of England Primary School, London, England; alexandra.hammond@st-georges.wandsworth.sch.uk; https://orcid.org/0000-0002-3834-797X

2. An explanation for terms followed by an asterisk can be found in the glossary: https://doi.org/10.14705/rpnet.2022.55.1367

3. https://www.compare-school-performance.service.gov.uk/school/101044/st-george's-cofe-primary-school/2021/absence-and-pupil-population

How to cite: Hammond, A. (2022). St George's Church of England Primary School, London, England. In A. Beaven, A. Comas-Quinn & N. Hinton (Eds), *Systematic synthetic phonics: case studies from Sounds-Write practitioners* (pp. 105-112). Research-publishing.net. https://doi.org/10.14705/rpnet.2022.55.1365

Pupils use this information to support the very strong spelling seen in their literacy work"[4].

2. Implementation

When I joined the Year 1 team in 2017, Sounds-Write was already well-established within the school from Reception to Year 6. I was trained in Sounds-Write straight away and was lucky enough to be mentored through my teaching by a Sounds-Write trainer and experienced teacher of early reading who had been working at the school for nearly 30 years.

Our Sounds-Write journey began in 2011. Spelling across the school was poor and it was clear that the phonics programme we were using was not working for us. In September 2011, all of the teaching staff and teaching assistants were trained in Sounds-Write and the programme was implemented throughout the school.

When new teachers arrive at St George's, they are enrolled onto the Sounds-Write face-to-face 4-day training course straightaway and are mentored by a more experienced member of staff, through team teaching and support with planning, until they are fully confident in teaching Sounds-Write. The way in which we mentor new members of staff includes observing the teachers regularly and giving them in-the-moment feedback. We also hold gallery lessons in different year groups for new members of staff to come and see, and we team teach with them for the first month or so when they start. Team teaching in phonics means that we plan and deliver the lesson together.

Sounds-Write also offers Continuous Professional Development (CPD) and support for the teachers and we often have one of the Sounds-Write trainers come into school and offer support and training. Since implementing the Sounds-Write programme, the school has seen dramatic improvements in reading, writing, and spelling outcomes for the children and in teachers' subject knowledge. We have

---

4. https://files.ofsted.gov.uk/v1/file/50055580

seen our Phonics Screening Check* results rise to between 96%-100% each year and the spelling in KS2 has greatly improved – this has been shown through our data from Young's *Parallel Spelling Tests**.

At St George's we teach Sounds-Write from the end of nursery through to Year 6. We teach the children as a whole class and provide interventions, where necessary, for those children who require extra support. In Year 1, where the children begin to learn the Extended Code, we have a specialist teacher who is able to take a small group of children that require more support and teach them the same content as the rest of the class but at a pace which suits them. The specialist teacher will take the children at the same time as the rest of the class are having their phonics lesson. This group of children does not always stay the same throughout the year – if a child becomes more confident during the lessons and we can see the progress in their written work, then we will put them back into class. Similarly, a child who has begun to need additional support in the whole class lesson will be moved to the small group that requires more support.

In this particular case study, I have taken Young's *Parallel Spelling Tests* data for one class and followed their spelling progress throughout their time at our primary school. The data includes their spelling data from Year 1 to Year 6 – omitting Year 5 data due to COVID-19 school closures. I have 20 students to comment on as I have excluded data for children who either left the school before Year 6 or who arrived later than Year 1.

Each child in this cohort has been taught phonics using the Sounds-Write programme from Reception through to Year 6. In Years 1 and 2, they were taught in two groups – one larger group was taught in the main classroom and a smaller group of seven or eight children were taught the same content by a specialist teacher at a pace more suitable for them. The smaller group was made up of children who had either SEND or English as an additional language. Children 4, 6, 8, 9, and 18 all have English as an additional language and were given extra one-to-one interventions whilst they were in KS1. In KS2, the same children were monitored closely during phonics lessons and taken for interventions as a small group when they were in Year 3 and 4.

Chapter 11

3. Evaluation

Using the Sounds-Write programme in our school has completely transformed the teaching and learning of phonics, and enabled our children to be successful readers and writers. We can see this across the school through our good level of development data, Phonics Screening Check results and Young's *Parallel Spelling Tests* data. Every class from Year 1 to Year 6 takes a test from Young's *Parallel Spelling Tests* in September and again in June. Table 1 shows Young's *Parallel Spelling Tests* data for the June spelling test taken by the same class from Year 1 to Year 6, and the progress made each year.

Table 1. Young's *Parallel Spelling Tests* data for the same cohort of children from Year 1 to Year 6

Child	Year 1 2016			Year 2 2017			Year 3 2018			Year 4 2019			Year 6 2021		
	Age	Spelling Age	Progress since Sept.	Age	Spelling Age	Progress since Sept.	Age	Spelling Age	Progress since Sept.	Age	Spelling Age	Progress since Sept.	Age	Spelling Age	Progress since Sept.
1	6.8	9.7	2.6	7.8	10.5	0.8	8.8	11.9	1.4	9.8	12.3	0.4	11.8	>15.0	+
2	6.6	9.9	3.3	7.6	11	1.1+	8.6	12.5	1.5	9.6	13.7	1.2	11.6	>15.0	+
3	6.4	7.7	1.8+	7.4	8.2	0.5	8.4	8.8	0.6	9.5	10.0	1.2	11.5	12.4	+1.4
4	6.3	6.7	0.6	7.3	7.5	0.8	8.3	7.7	0.2	9.3	7.9	0.2	11.3	9.0	+0.1
5	6.9	9.0	1.9	7.9	9.3	0.3	8.9	12.5	3.2	9.9	12.7	0.2	11.10	>15.0	+>1.1
6	6.0	7.7	1.0	7.0	7.8	0.1	8.0	8.6	0.8	9.0	9.0	0.4	11.0	9.8	0.5
7	6.6	8.1	1.6	7.6	9.7	1.6	8.6	11.9	2.2	9.6	13.7	1.8	11.7	>15.0	+
8	6.3	7.4	0.8	7.3	7.7	0.3	8.3	8.1	0.4	9.3	10.7	2.6	11.3	8.6	+0.4
9	5.10	7.7	1.6	6.10	8.5	0.8	7.10	9.1	0.6	8.10	10.0	0.9	10.10	10.8	+1.0
10	6.3	8.5	2.0	7.3	9.5	1.0	8.3	11.1	1.6	9.3	13.2	2.1	11.3	>15.0	+
11	6.1	7.8	1.3	7.1	8.5	0.7	8.1	10.2	1.7	9.1	10.4	0.2	11.2	11.4	0
12	5.11	7.5	0.9	6.11	9.7	2.2	7.11	11.1	1.4	8.11	13.2	2.1	10.11	>15.0	+>2.1
13	6.3	7.8	1.1	7.3	9.9	2.1	8.3	10.2	0.3	9.3	11.4	1.2	11.3	13.5	0
14	6.1	8.0	1.1	7.1	9.0	1.0	8.1	10	1.0	9.1	10.3	0.3	11.1	14.4	+2.0
15	6.7	9.7	2.7	7.7	10.5	0.8	8.6	11.4	0.9	9.7	13.7	2.3	11.7	>15.0	+
16	6.4	8.5	1.1	7.5	9.3	0.8	8.4	11.1	1.8	9.4	12.0	0.9	11.5	14.4	+1.2
17	6.7	7.7	1.1	7.7	8.6	0.9	8.7	10	1.4	9.7	10.7	0.7	11.7	11.6	+0.2
18	6.2	7.5	0.9	7.2	8.2	0.7	8.2	9.4	1.2	9.2	9.8	0.5	11.2	10.8	+1.0
19	6.1	8.2	1.3	7.2	9.9	1.7	8.1	12.5	2.6	9.2	13.7	1.2	11.2	15.0	1.8
20	6.9	8.5	1.9	7.9	8.6	0.1	8.9	10.8	2.2	9.9	12.0	1.2	11.9	13.5	+1.9

Table 1 shows the progress in spelling for 20 children over five years at our school. All of the children have made good progress, with many children making significant progress during that time. Looking at the results for each year, you can see that every child's spelling age increased consistently from the September spelling test to the June spelling test. In Year 1, all of the children had a spelling age which was higher than their chronological age and they all made huge progress during this year – this was the year when they learned most of the Extended Code. This continued into Year 2 – with 85% of children making between 0.5 and 2.2 years' progress from Year 1 to Year 2. As a result of this, all of the children passed the Phonics Screening Check in Year 1 and were fluent readers by the end of KS1.

In KS2, all children continued to make progress during each academic year with at least 90% starting the year with a higher spelling age than their chronological age. Even though some children may have only made what seems like a small amount of progress for the academic year, it is important to also look at their spelling age in comparison to their chronological age – for example, Child 1 made 0.34 years progress in Year 4 but their spelling age was 12.3, in comparison to their chronological age of 9.8.

The children who had interventions in KS1 and KS2 (Child 4, 6, 8, 9, and 18) seem to show little progress between Year 4 and Year 6. This is due to the effects of lockdowns and remote learning. Those children were targeted for online tutoring by their class teachers, however, lack of internet, computers, a quiet learning space at home, and engagement with online learning all stood as barriers to the children's progress. Once provided with a device which had internet access, engagement with home learning was still a struggle. The majority of students, however, still made huge progress despite the difficulties of home learning.

From as early as Year 1, when we begin to teach the Extended Code, we see an increase in confidence in the children's independent writing from using the Sounds-Write programme. Children from a young age are able to segment the word that they want to write into the correct sounds and use the sound-spelling correspondences that they know to write the word. They are also confident enough to ask which spelling of a certain sound is the one that is used in the word they are trying to write. Our use of phonics displays in every classroom enables children to become more independent in their writing, with children and teachers referring to them whenever they are writing. In KS2, the children use the strategies they have learned in the polysyllabic lessons to write words independently.

Despite the struggles that the children have faced over the past two years, by the end of Year 6, 69% of children had a spelling age that was higher than their chronological age. In comparison to national data, 36% of students met the higher standard for grammar, punctuation, and spelling in the 2018/19 Year 6 national tests. These results have enabled the children to leave primary school and move onto secondary school as confident readers, writers, and spellers. The teachers can all feel confident that they have each made a positive impact on all of the children's reading and spelling over their primary school career and the results are a testament to the school's high expectations for teaching and learning.

Table 2. Phonics Screening Check – % passing

Year	2014	2015	2016	2017	2018	2019
National results	74%	77%	81%	81%	82%	82%
St George's results	100%	100%	100%	100%	97%	93%

The results from the Phonics Screening Check, as shown in Table 2, are a real testament to the Sounds-Write programme. The majority of our children pass the screening check with a score of 40/40 and enter Year 2 as fluent readers. In 2018 and 2019, we had a small number of children who had SEND and although they made excellent progress during Year 1, they were unable to pass the Phonics Screening Check. Despite this, our results were still considerably higher than the national average for both years.

Table 3 shows that the percentage of children at St George's achieving a good level of development for literacy (comprehension, reading, and writing) at the end of Reception has increased from 2016 to present, and our results are consistently higher than the national average. This is due to the comprehensive programme that Sounds-Write provides for teaching the Initial Code in the Early Years.

Table 3. Good level of development at the end of Reception

Year	2016	2017	2018	2019
National results	69.3%	70.7%	71.5%	71.8%
St George's results	71%	83%	80%	80%

4. Recommendations

Our experience at St George's has shown the importance of training all staff in Sounds-Write, including teaching assistants, in order to ensure consistency and fidelity to the programme throughout the school. In ensuring that all staff are fully trained, it also means that there is more capacity in school to deliver interventions to those children who require additional support. We often use our most experienced teaching assistants to deliver any extra interventions – especially for children who are new to the country or who have English as an additional language. These interventions are delivered in the afternoons in KS1 and in KS2 we either bring the children into school slightly earlier or hold a session after school. The class teacher is responsible for planning all of the sessions, even if they are not always delivering them. They will then liaise with the adult who is delivering the session to monitor the children's progress. The content of the sessions will be based on what the teacher knows the child needs more support with from what they have seen in the phonics lessons. Weekly spelling tests and half-term grammar, punctuation, and spelling tests are used to track the children's progress, as well as their independent writing.

Having a member of staff lead and support phonics in school has been essential to the success of the Sounds-Write programme, especially with KS2 where phonics is not traditionally a focus and teachers do not feel as confident in their teaching of it. We have found that good quality CPD resources provided by Sounds-Write have helped tremendously in developing teacher subject knowledge and confidence in teaching the polysyllabic word lessons in particular.

In order to maximise the impact of Sounds-Write in the children's writing, each classroom has a phonics display which is updated with each new sound that the children learn. This acts as a fantastic reference point for the children during their Sounds-Write lessons. If it is an unfamiliar word, they will often ask which spelling of a certain sound is in a word that they are writing and the teacher will use the display to point to the correct one. When a child is faced with spelling an unfamiliar word, especially in KS2, their knowledge of breaking words into syllables from the polysyllabic lessons provides the children with strategies to attempt to write words that they would usually shy away from. Each child has a whiteboard at their table and we encourage them to try and write an unfamiliar word there first before they write it in their books.

At St George's we have also found that using the Sounds-Write reading books in conjunction with the programme has had a huge impact on our children's reading levels. Each child in Reception and KS1 reads with an adult every day and they take a book home every night. The expectation from us is that they read with an adult at home for 15 minutes every night and we will change the book the next day. We have found that the combination of Sounds-Write lessons and guided reading sessions every day, where a Sounds-Write trained adult is using all of the language and error corrections from the programme, has enabled the children to make incredible progress throughout the early years and KS1.

We also hold family learning sessions every half term to teach the parents the strategies we use at school to teach their children. There is always a phonics, a reading, and a writing family learning over the year. During these sessions we encourage the parents to complete the free Sounds-Write Course for parents and carers and we share a link with them which shows them how to pronounce the pure sounds precisely.

At St George's, to further refine our practice, we are continuing to train our staff by booking them onto the new Sounds-Write CPD sessions, such as the Year 3 to 6 course, the masterclasses, and the planning webinars.

12. The Pavilion School, Melbourne, Australia

Naomi Stockley[1], Rianna Tatana[2], Roshni Kaur[3], Alice Reynolds[4]

1. Context

The Pavilion School is located in Melbourne, Australia. It is a specialist Flexible Learning Option (FLO) for students who have disengaged or been excluded from mainstream education. There are 235 secondary-aged school students enrolled across two campuses in Melbourne's northern suburbs. A considerable proportion of students at the Pavilion School face significant risk factors which impede their access to education. They are as follows: mental health challenges (60% of students); alcohol and other drug use (49%); school absenteeism (47%); family vulnerability (47%); and youth justice involvement (16%).

Other relevant demographics that make up our student population include the following: 25% receive funding as part of the Program for Students with Disabilities (PSD); 24% identify as Aboriginal and Torres Strait Islander; and 10% are in Out of Home Care.

The school uses a trauma-informed model that supports students' educational goals in tandem with their social development. Students are enrolled in class groups of fifteen to twenty and each group is assigned a dedicated classroom

---

1. The Pavilion School, Melbourne, Australia; naomi.stockley@education.vic.gov.au

2. The Pavilion School, Melbourne, Australia; rianna.tatana@education.vic.gov.au

3. The Pavilion School, Melbourne, Australia; roshni.kaur@education.vic.gov.au

4. The Pavilion School, Melbourne, Australia; alice.reynolds@education.vic.gov.au

How to cite: Stockley, N., Tatana, R., Kaur, R., & Reynolds, A. (2022). The Pavilion School, Melbourne, Australia. In A. Beaven, A. Comas-Quinn & N. Hinton (Eds), *Systematic synthetic phonics: case studies from Sounds-Write practitioners* (pp. 113-123). Research-publishing.net. https://doi.org/10.14705/rpnet.2022.55.1366

and staff 'triad' comprising a teacher, wellbeing worker, and education support worker, who collaborate to support students' learning and wellbeing. Students have a reduced timetable and access to a range of onsite services, including counseling, drug and alcohol support, the Doctors in Schools Program[5], occupational therapy, and speech pathology.

Classroom teachers provide instruction across the six strands of the Victorian Certificate of Applied Learning and differentiate to support students to develop fundamental literacy, numeracy, and social and emotional learning skills. The teaching and learning model draws on evidence-based practices, emphasizing explicit direct instruction and with a focus on structured literacy teaching practices.

The Sounds-Write school phonics program was implemented at the start of 2021, with the aim of establishing a structured whole-school approach to providing phonics intervention. Interventions and additional support were previously provided to students largely at classroom level. The Response to Intervention (RTI) framework within a Multi-Tiered System of Support[*6] (MTSS), is a proactive structure for providing instruction and intervention across the school (see Figure 1). The integrated instruction model of MTSS uses collected data to assess student needs and provide them with interventions in appropriate tiers. It begins in the general classroom (Tier 1) and increases in intensity in subsequent tiers. The aim of implementing this program across the school was to effectively support students at Tier 3 level (intensive support delivered at a one-to-one level) using the RTI framework.

This case study will provide insights into the implementation and early-stage impacts of the Sounds-Write school phonics program, with a focus on providing recommendations for improvement and insights that will support other educators to establish effective whole-school intervention programs in flexible and alternative settings for vulnerable secondary students.

---

5. A Victorian state government initiative funding general practitioners to attend government schools, providing advice and healthcare to students most in need.

6. An explanation for terms followed by an asterisk can be found in the glossary: https://doi.org/10.14705/rpnet.2022.55.1367

Figure 1. RTI[7]

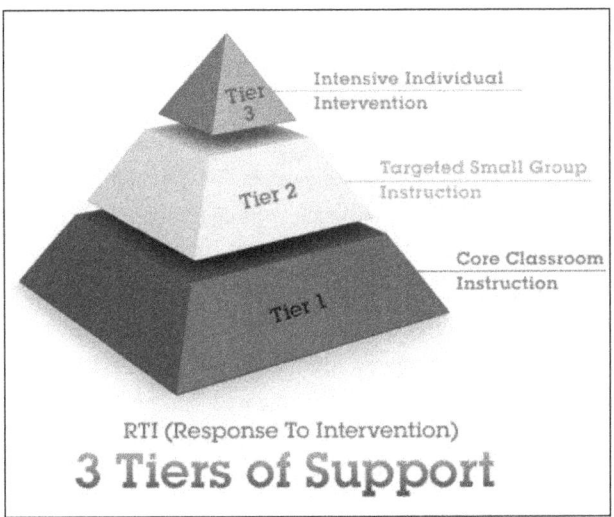

2. Implementation

Over a period of 24 months (2018-2020), all teachers at the Pavilion School were trained in Sounds-Write to provide intensive one-to-one intervention, small group, and whole class spelling lessons, with additional support in assessment and therapy provided by two speech pathologists. As of 2021, all but two new teachers had been trained in Sounds-Write, six in person and three online.

Sounds-Write skills tests and code knowledge tests indicated that students across the school had significant gaps in the fundamental skills and knowledge required for reading and spelling. This is reflective of wider research: adolescents in FLO settings typically have weak oral language skills and poor reading comprehension (less than twelve years) when compared with their like age peers (Snow, Graham,

---

7. https://www.education.vic.gov.au/school/teachers/classrooms/Pages/aproacheseppdiff.aspx#link1

McLean, & Serry, 2020[8]), as well as higher than typical levels of undiagnosed developmental language difficulties (Snow, McLean, & Frederico, 2020[9]).

In 2021, teachers began providing additional one-to-one intervention to students identified as high priority through the analysis of various sets of assessments. The Test of Word Reading Efficiency – Second Edition (TOWRE-2) was used as an initial standardized screening assessment. This encompasses two sub-tests: Sight-Word Efficiency and Phonemic Decoding Efficiency. Students identified as being below average for Phonemic Decoding Efficiency were then assessed using the Sounds-Write skills tests and code knowledge test. Testing was carried out by classroom teachers with the support of the team's instructional coach and the two school speech pathologists. Students were then selected for one-to-one intervention based on an analysis of highest need and highest attendance. This was especially necessary given the limited school resources and teacher time capacity to provide intervention outside classroom hours.

Students selected for intervention ranged in age from fourteen to eighteen and either required intervention starting at Initial Code* or the early stages of Extended Code*. Sounds-Write instruction for one-to-one intervention was delivered face-to-face except during COVID-19 lockdowns, which necessitated a move to online intervention using the Sounds-Write Smart Notebook tools.

TOWRE-2 and Sounds-Write data continues to be used at classroom level to provide small group and whole class instruction and will form part of the next phase of phonics intervention (see Recommendations for further details). The focus in the first year of implementation was to support frequent and consistent Tier 3 intervention in order to meet students at their most significant point of need. The evaluation data will focus on students who have been receiving intervention since the start of 2021.

---

8. Snow, P. C., Graham, L. J., Mclean, E. J., & Serry, T. A. (2020). The oral language and reading comprehension skills of adolescents in flexible learning programmes. *International Journal of Speech-Language Pathology, 22*(4), 425-434. https://doi.org/10.1080/17549507.2019.165403

9. Snow, P., McLean, E., & Frederico, M. (2020). The language, literacy and mental health profiles of adolescents in out-of-home care: an Australian sample. *Child Language Teaching and Therapy, 36*(3), 151-163. https://doi.org/10.1177/0265659020940360

3. Evaluation

The data in Table 1 shows that for students receiving Tier 3 intervention, TOWRE-2 scaled scores have increased by an average of three scaled scores over a six-month period. For many students, the impact of complex contextual factors is important to consider – see details in the evaluation below.

Table 1. Scaled scores: the Sight-Word Efficiency and Phonemic Decoding Efficiency scaled scores are combined to create the Total Word Reading Efficiency scaled scores

Student	Intervention sessions attended (as of 5th August 2021)	Sub-test Sight-Word efficiency RD1 - Feb 21	Sub-test Phonemic Decoding Efficiency RD1	Total Word Reading Efficiency (TWRE) RD 1	Sub-test Sight-Word efficiency RD2 - July 21	Sub-test Phonemic Decoding Efficiency RD2	Total Word Reading Efficiency (TWRE) RD 2	Change in TOWRE Scores	Change in %ile rank
A	10	76	62	67	72	71	79	12	1
B	13	84	65	73	84	87	85	12	12
C	1	77	62	68	75	62	67	-1	0
D	14	73	63	66	68	63	64	-2	0
E	14	76	69	71	80	75	76	5	2
F	3	70	56	61	74	55	63	2	0.5
G	3	91	88	89	90	82	85	-4	-7
H	5	81	76	77	79	74	75	-2	-1
I	30	55	55	53	55	55	53	0	0
J	8	81	76	76	82	72	76	0	0
Average	10	76	67	69	76	70	72	3	1

Classification of Skills	Very Poor	Poor	Below Average	Average	Above Average
Scaled Score	<70	70-79	80-89	90-110	111-120

Chapter 12

In analyzing the data in Table 1, some contextual factors must be considered, including the specific challenges facing the Pavilion School cohort and the disproportionately negative impact of COVID-19 lockdowns on many of our students and their families. Specifically, the following conclusions are drawn from comparing TOWRE-2 data from February and July/August 2021. Originally, the phonics team planned to reassess students using the Sounds Skills and Code Knowledge tests during this time, however due to the impact of the August lockdown, this was not achieved for all students. Where possible and relevant, Sounds-Write assessment data has been included to provide further detail into the analysis of student results. Further analysis after a longer period of implementation will be required to determine long-term, whole-school impact.

Of students who received intervention, their TOWRE-2 scaled scores have increased by an average of three scaled scores over a six-month period. This is promising, particularly given attendance challenges across our cohort, which means many students only attended an average of nine sessions overall. Further, TOWRE-2 measures students against aged norm averages. Students who do not score within the average bracket means their combined Sight-Word Efficiency and Phonemic Decoding Skills are significantly below their peers within the same age range. As a result, scaled scores can be impacted due to students moving up an age bracket in the second round of testing. Despite this, in some cases, students' scaled scores have increased. This scaled score provides a precise estimate of the extent to which the students' performance is different from the average of other students at the same age level. Particular attention should be paid to Students B, E, I, and J, who reflect the impact of various individual contextual factors on results.

Firstly, Student B has a diagnosed developmental language disorder. Despite these additional challenges, they showed significant growth by progressing from a TOWRE scaled score of 73 (poor range) to a TOWRE scaled score of 85 (below average), following a six-month period of one-to-one intervention. What is of particular significance is Student B's increase in Phonemic Decoding Efficiency, which progressed from a score of 65 (very poor) to 87 (below average).

Student B has attended intervention sessions inconsistently, receiving a total of thirteen sessions during this time. The results are extremely encouraging given that the work of Snow, McLean, and Frederico (2020) demonstrate that such language difficulties have a higher-than-normal prevalence among vulnerable cohorts such as that of the students at the Pavilion School.

During the second round of testing, Student E moved up an age bracket. Despite this, and inconsistent intervention sessions due to periods of remote learning, Student E still showed improvement in Phonemic Decoding Efficiency, progressing from 69 (very poor) to 75 (poor) in the TOWRE-2. We suspect that Student E's progress was enabled by their motivated attitude toward receiving intervention and their consistent attendance with normal classes. In addition, their willingness to consistently complete follow-up weekly tasks for each session allowed Student E to consolidate skills introduced during intervention sessions.

In the case of some students who have shown negative progress or no progress, several complex factors need to be considered. One interpretation of the results could be students engaging with intervention may still be consolidating their skills and have not yet transferred code knowledge to long-term memory. This is because they have not had enough exposure to new symbols and sounds to transfer them to their long-term memory for quick retrieval. This has also been impacted by COVID-19 lockdowns as students have been less able to use retrieval practice. Research indicates that for older students with severe reading difficulties, it is difficult for them to make extremely rapid progress in a short amount of time.

Student I attended 30 intervention sessions. However, they show no growth in their TOWRE-2 score between assessment rounds. This student has nevertheless progressed four units through the Sounds-Write program. They can now read sentences containing previously taught code accurately and fluently, including decoding some two-syllable words. Student I began intervention through the whole-school program at Unit 8 of Initial Code, and at the time of the second round of assessments had just completed Unit 11. As the TOWRE-2 assessment moves rapidly from Initial Code to Extended Code words in the Phonemic Decoding Test, it does not reflect this progress. It does however become apparent when comparing their TOWRE-2 data with their Sounds-Write data (Table 2), which is more sensitive and thus highlights the progress they have made through the Sounds-Write units.

Table 2.   Student I Sounds-Write assessment data

Round 1	Segmenting	7
	Blending	2
	Phoneme Manipulation	1
	Code Knowledge	13
Round 2	Segmenting	50
	Blending	5
	Phoneme Manipulation	6
	Code Knowledge	29

Student I increased across all four assessments, with an especially significant increase in their segmenting skills – suggesting a significantly increased phonemic awareness of language – and code knowledge (Table 2).

Table 3.   Student J Sounds-Write data

Round 1	Segmenting	65
	Blending	10
	Phoneme Manipulation	4
	Code Knowledge	31
Round 2	Segmenting	66
	Blending	12
	Phoneme Manipulation	6
	Code Knowledge	39

Student J was measured against a higher age bracket during the second round of testing. Student J started on Unit 5 of Sounds-Write and they are now at Unit 11 of Initial Code, and their Sounds-Write data shows a slight increase in skills, and a moderate increase in code knowledge (Table 3). Similarly to Student I, the TOWRE-2 does not reveal the full story of their progress. TOWRE-2 includes many words containing sound-spelling correspondences from the Extended Code that Student J has not learned yet. Additionally, J's general cognitive ability is within the 'very low' range of intellectual functioning (Full Scale Intelligence Quotient or FSIQ*: 72). These are significant barriers for Student J that are not captured within standardized forms of testing. J also has specific mental health challenges and occupies a caregiver role at home, which means they are unable to engage effectively with learning during remote learning periods.

4. Recommendations

We offer the following recommendations/considerations to fellow Sounds-Write educators and practitioners based on our experience of implementing this program thus far.

- Train all teaching staff in Sounds-Write. This develops the capacity of all teachers and ensures a consistent approach to teaching decoding and encoding skills across classes.

- Use online software such as MS OneNote to collate all program resources and lesson records. This assists with the effective sharing of resources, and consistency and efficiency when planning Sounds-Write lessons.

- Develop a universal lesson template for Initial and Extended Code lessons (see example in supplementary materials[10]). These provide a template for planning and recording Sounds-Write lessons, and have been especially supportive for teachers new to the program with less experience planning and delivering lessons.

- Carefully consider the selection process for students who will be receiving intervention. We selected students based on highest need and highest attendance. We have adjusted our program so that now each staff member involved is working with no more than two students, allowing

---

10. https://research-publishing.box.com/s/ehtsw5abpom351sd0ll05y9tb1ye2qj1

Chapter 12

for more intense intervention. This is particularly important when working with students who have significant attendance challenges, as it provides greater opportunities for engagement.

- Ensure careful and detailed analysis of learning and assessment data. Analysis should consider the following factors while conducting intervention:

  - Complexity of students' needs – neurodevelopmental disorders, learning and/or language difficulties, mental health difficulties (childhood trauma, anxiety disorders etc.), and other comorbidities.

  - Implications and limitations of standardized assessments such as the TOWRE-2 – for example, reading words within a specified time limit.

  - A change in chronological age when completing the post assessment (as we are using the age-based normative table to obtain the scaled scores).

- Regular phonics team meetings to evaluate student progress and attendance. This has been crucial given the significant need for Tier 3 (intensive one-to-one) intervention in our student cohort. Student data is organized based on need and attendance. If students miss more than three sessions in a row without reasonable explanation, they are replaced with a student of next highest need until their attendance increases in consistency.

Additionally, we would ideally make the following adjustments in the next phase of implementing our phonics program.

- Train education support staff in Sounds-Write. This would not only mean we could provide more students with one-to-one intervention but would further increase the capacity of our staff teams in providing specialized one-on-one support to students in class.

- Provide some teachers time release from other duties to support consistent and intensive intervention. Again, this would allow us to reach a greater number of students across our cohort, and assist in managing attendance challenges.

- Provide ongoing support to the teaching team to ensure Tier 1 and 2 intervention is being carried out consistently. Ongoing collaborative planning and modeling of lessons to teachers trained in Sounds-Write but not involved in one-to-one intervention sessions will support regular and targeted implementation of Sounds-Write at classroom level.

We would also again highlight the challenges of collecting student data during a pandemic – particularly with a vulnerable student cohort – and hope to consolidate our data collection and recording processes across the coming year.

Establishing a structured whole-school approach to providing phonics intervention in a year when the COVID-19 pandemic has had such an impact on schooling has presented additional challenges alongside those that typically arise in a FLO context. Our team has been able to establish a framework for assessment, referral, and tiered implementation of the Sounds-Write program that has already begun to see some incremental success for students. We anticipate that over time, we will see lastly impacts of the program on student outcomes, equipping them with fundamental literacy skills.

Glossary

Academy (UK)
    Academies receive funding directly from the government and are run by an academy trust. They have more control over how they do things than community schools. Academies do not charge fees.

Dibels
    The Dynamic Indicators of Basic Early Literacy Skills (https://dibels.uoregon.edu/about-dibels) is a set of indicators that measure literacy during pre-school and primary school, based on short, regularly administered tests that provide a longitudinal evaluation of progress.

Dyslexia-SPELD Foundation (Australia)
    The Dyslexia-SPELD Foundation (DSF) is an independent, not-for-profit organisation that provides a range of services for individuals with persistent learning difficulties and disorders (https://dsf.net.au/).

Education Assistants (Australia)
    Classroom assistants who support the class teacher.

Education, Health, and Care Plan (England and Wales)
    An Education, Health, and Care Plan (EHCP) is for children and young people aged up to 25 who need more support than is available through special educational needs support. EHCPs identify educational, health, and social needs and set out additional support to meet those needs.

English Language Learners (ELL)
    Students in the US who are unable to communicate fluently in English, usually because they come from non-English-speaking homes and backgrounds, and who typically require specialised instruction (https://www.edglossary.org/english-language-learner/). In the UK, these correspond to English as an Additional Language (EAL).

---

1. **How to cite:** Beaven, A., Comas-Quinn, A., & Hinton, N. (2022). Glossary. In A. Beaven, A. Comas-Quinn & N. Hinton (Eds), *Systematic synthetic phonics: case studies from Sounds-Write practitioners* (pp. 125-129). Research-publishing.net. https://doi.org/10.14705/rpnet.2022.55.1367

Glossary

Extended Code

After introducing students to the Initial Code, teachers move onto the most common ways to spell the more complex two-, three-, or four-letter spellings. This is called the Extended Code, which further develops the skills and the conceptual understanding of how the writing system works.

Form (UK)

The term is used in phrases such as single-form/two-form entry to refer to how many classes there are per year-group.

Foundation (Australia)

Also called Pre-Primary. Children turning five by 30th June.

Free School Meals (England and Wales)

Children in state-funded schools in England and Wales are entitled to receive free school meals if a parent or carer is in receipt of certain income-related benefits. Children remain eligible until they finish the phase of schooling (primary or secondary). The percentage of free school meals is used as an indicator of the socio-economic background of families in a school.

Good Level of Development (UK)

Good Level of Development (GLD) is a measure of development for children in the Early Years Foundation Stage (EYFS). Children are defined as having reached a GLD at the end of the EYFS if they achieve at least the 'expected' level in: personal, social, and emotional development; physical development; communication and language; mathematics; and literacy.

Index of Community Socio-Educational Advantage (Australia)

The Index of Community Socio-Educational Advantage (ICSEA) was developed to enable fair and meaningful comparisons between schools of the students' performance in literacy and numeracy as

Glossary

estimated by the National Assessment Program – Literacy and Numeracy (NAPLAN) based on the level of educational advantage or disadvantage that students bring to their academic studies. ICSEA values are calculated on a scale which has a median of 1,000 and a standard deviation of 100.

Initial Code

In Sounds-Write, teachers start by teaching the most common sound-spelling correspondences represented by single letters, as well as some of the most common digraphs – this is called the Initial Code. The Initial Code also includes the teaching of the skills and the beginning of conceptual understanding of how the writing system works.

Key Stages (England)

The National Curriculum in England is organised into blocks of years called 'Key Stages'. Key Stage 1 is the first block, consisting of Year 1 and Year 2. Key Stage 2 is the second block, consisting of Years 3, 4, 5, and 6. Lower Key Stage 2 (LKS2) refers to Year 3 and 4, and Upper Key Stage 2 (UKS2) refers to Years 5 and 6.

Kindergarten/Kindy (Australia)

Kindergartens are for children turning four by 30th June, attending the year before Pre-Primary (first year of school).

Local Deprivation Factor (UK)

The Indices of Deprivation are a unique measure of relative deprivation at a small local area level across England. The indices provide a set of relative measures of deprivation based on seven different domains: income, employment, education, skills and training, health deprivation and disability, crime, barriers to housing and services, and living environment. Areas are ranked on an index (100-0), with higher indices being the more deprived areas (https://assets.publishing.service.gov.uk/government/uploads/system/uploads/attachment_data/file/853811/IoD2019_FAQ_v4.pdf).

Glossary

NAPLAN (Australia)
NAPLAN is an annual national assessment for all students in Years 3, 5, 7, and 9. All students in these year levels are expected to participate in tests in reading, writing, language conventions (spelling, grammar, and punctuation) and numeracy (https://www.nap.edu.au/naplan/faqs/naplan--general).

OFSTED (England)
OFSTED is the Office for Standards in Education, Children's Services and Skills. They inspect services which provide education and skills for learners of all ages (https://www.gov.uk/government/organisations/ofsted/about).

Phonics Screening Check (England)
The Phonics Screening Check (PSC) is a statutory test for all Year 1 pupils in England, designed to assess their ability to decode new words. The test includes both real and pseudo words.

Pre-Primary (Australia)
Children turning five by 30th June.

Pupil Premium Grant (UK)
The Pupil Premium Grant (PPG) provides funding to enable disadvantaged pupils of all abilities to reach their potential, and supports children and young people with parents in the regular armed forces.

Response to Intervention (RTI) framework
An RTI framework consists of monitoring student progress in response to the instruction and interventions, and using these measures to shape further instruction.

SATs (England)
SATs are standardised assessment tests administered by primary schools in England to children in Year 2 and Year 6 to check their educational

Glossary

progress. They are one marker used by the government, and hence parents, of the quality of the education at a school.

Scope and sequence (Australia)
A scope and sequence is the summary of the syllabus, the sequence in which content will be taught and the intended learning outcomes.

SEND (Special Education Needs and Disabilities)
A student has special educational needs if they have a learning difficulty and/or a disability that means they need special health and education support. This is often shortened to SEND.

Tier 1, Tier 2, Tier 3
Tiers are part of the response to RTI frameworks, which consists in monitoring student progress in response to instruction, and using these measures to shape further instruction. Tier 1 involves whole-class instruction. Tier 2 intervention involves small group instruction for those struggling at Tier 1. Tier 3 is the most intense level of RTI (https://www.understood.org/articles/en/3-tiers-of-rti-support).

Transiency
The degree to which students change schools throughout their compulsory education, beyond the change from primary to secondary school.

Young's *Parallel Spelling Tests*
A set of parallel spelling tests which are designed to chart children's progress in spelling from age six to thirteen years.

Whole Language Approach to Reading
This refers to a collection of approaches and strategies that focus on learners memorising an increasing number of whole words.

Author index

B
Beaven, Ana v
Beaven, Tita v, 1

C
Comas-Quinn, Anna v

D
Darwin, Emma vi, 8, 87

E
Eichhorn, Katie vi, 7, 55

G
Gilbert, Kathy vi, 7, 55

H
Hall, Myra vi, 7, 55
Hammond, Alexandra vi, 8, 105
Hammond, Kendall vii, 8, 71
Harley, Anita vii, 8, 79
Helsloot, Angela vii, 7, 11
Hinton, Naomi v
Hornberger, Shelley vii, 8, 97
Horner, Sarah vii, 7, 31

J
Jones, Tracy vii, 8, 63

K
Kaur, Roshni vii, 9, 113

L
Lawyer, Gretchen viii, 7, 55

M
MacKechnie, Charlotte viii, 7, 23
McLean, Emina viii, 7, 43

N
Nunez, Jill viii, 7, 55

O
Orr, Jane viii, 7, 31

R
Reynolds, Alice ix, 9, 113

S
Snow, Pamela v, xv
Stockley, Naomi ix, 9, 113

T
Tatana, Rianna ix, 9, 113

W
Walker, John ix, 1

www.ingramcontent.com/pod-product-compliance
Lightning Source LLC
Chambersburg PA
CBHW031632160426
43196CB00006B/387